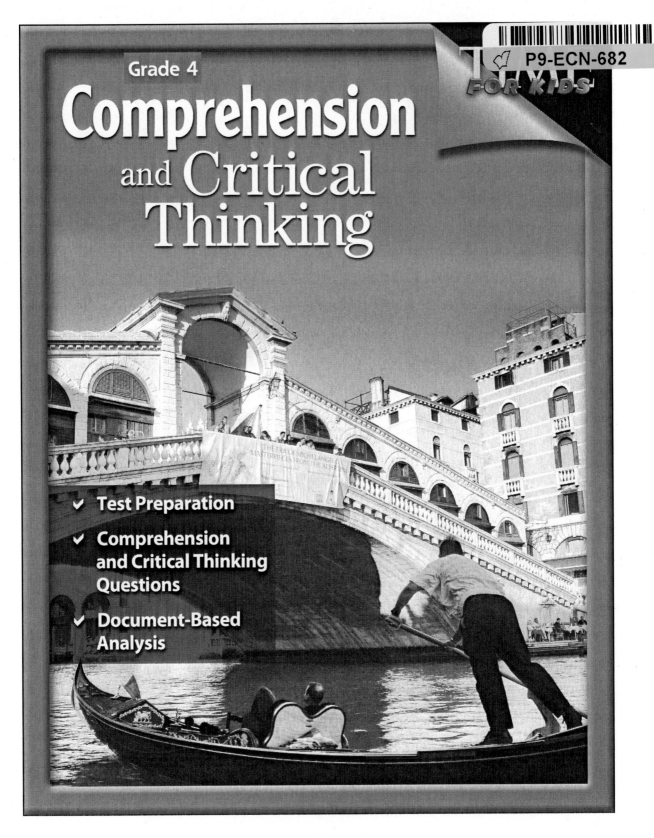

Grade 4

Comprehension
and Critical
Thinking

TIME FOR KIDS

- ✓ **Test Preparation**
- ✓ **Comprehension and Critical Thinking Questions**
- ✓ **Document-Based Analysis**

Author

Lisa Greathouse

The articles in this book are collected from the TIME For Kids archives.

SHELL EDUCATION

Editor
Jodene Lynn Smith, M.A.

Compiler
Maria Elvira Gallardo, M.A.

Assistant Editor
Leslie Huber, M.A.

Katie Das

Editorial Director
Dona Herweck Rice

Editor-in-Chief
Sharon Coan, M.S.Ed.

Editorial Manager
Gisela Lee, M.A.

Creative Director
Lee Aucoin

Cover Image
Compilation from Shutterstock.com

Illustration Manager
Timothy J. Bradley

Artist
Mira Fraser

Interior Layout Designer
Don Tran

Publisher
Corinne Burton, M.A.Ed.

Standards Compendium, Copyright 2004 McREL

Shell Education

5301 Oceanus Drive
Huntington Beach, CA 92649
http://www.shelleducation.com
ISBN 978-1-4258-0244-8
© 2008 Shell Educational Publishing, Inc.
Reprinted 2013

Table of Contents

Introduction and Research

Comprehension is the primary goal of any reading task. According to the RAND Reading Study Group, comprehension is "the process of simultaneously extracting and constructing meaning through interaction and involvement with written language" (2002, 11). Students who comprehend what they read have more opportunities in life, as well as better test performance. In order for students to become proficient readers, it is necessary that they are taught comprehension strategies such as predicting, monitoring comprehension, summarizing, visualizing, questioning, making connections, and inferring meaning (Miller 2002; Pardo 2002).

Focus on reading comprehension has become more urgent in light of NCLB legislation and emphasis on standardized testing. Because the majority of text found on standardized tests is nonfiction (Grigg, Daane, Jin, & Campbell 2003), teachers are now finding a greater need to teach skills using informational texts. For this reason, *Comprehension and Critical Thinking* provides teachers with informational texts in the form of articles about the contemporary world, as well as the past.

Research suggests that students need preparation in order to be successful on standardized tests. Gulek states: "Adequate and appropriate test preparation plays an important role in helping students demonstrate their knowledge and skills in high-stakes testing situations" (2003, 42). This preparation includes, among other things, teaching content and test-taking skills. Skills practiced when using the articles in *Comprehension and Critical Thinking* provide an excellent foundation for improving students' test-taking abilities.

Not only is reading nonfiction texts beneficial for testing purposes, but studies also show that students actually prefer informational texts. A 1998 study by Kletzien that focused on children's preferences for reading material indicated that younger children chose nonfiction text close to half the time when choosing their own reading materials. Similar studies (Ivey & Broaddus 2000; Moss & Hendershot 2002) revealed that older children prefer nonfiction and find greater motivation when reading informational texts.

In this book, each nonfiction passage includes a document-based question similar to trends in standardized testing. The students respond to a critical-thinking question based on the information gleaned from a given document. This document is related to the passage it accompanies. Document-based questions show a student's ability to apply prior knowledge and his or her capacity to transfer knowledge to a new situation. The activities are time efficient, allowing students to practice these skills every week. To yield the best results, such practice must begin at the start of the school year.

Students will need to use test-taking skills and strategies throughout their lives. The exercises in *Comprehension and Critical Thinking* will guide your students to become better readers and test takers. After practicing the exercises in this book, you will be pleased with your students' comprehension performance not only on standardized tests, but also with any expository text they encounter within the classroom and beyond its walls.

Objectives

All lessons in this book are designed to support the following objectives.

The students will:

- answer who, what, where, why, when, and how questions about the article
- support answers with information found in the article
- support answers with information inferred from the article
- support answers with information based on prior knowledge
- identify the main ideas in the article
- identify supporting details in the article
- draw conclusions based on information learned in the article
- make predictions based on information learned in the article
- form and defend an opinion based on information learned in the article
- respond to questions in written form

Readability

All of the reading passages included in this book have a 4.0–4.9 reading level based on the Flesch-Kincaid Readability Formula. This formula determines a readability level by calculating the number of words, syllables, and sentences.

Preparing Students to Read Nonfiction Text

One of the best ways to prepare students to read expository text is to read a short selection aloud daily. Reading expository text aloud is critical to developing your students' abilities to read it themselves. Because making predictions is another way to help students tap into their prior knowledge, read the beginning of a passage, then stop and ask the students to predict what might occur next. Do this at several points throughout your reading of the text. By doing this over time, you will find that your students' abilities to make accurate predictions greatly increases.

Of course, talking about nonfiction concepts is also very important. However, remember that discussion can never replace actually reading nonfiction texts because people rarely speak using the vocabulary and complex sentence structures of written language.

Asking questions helps students, especially struggling readers, to focus on what is important in a text. Also, remember the significance of wait time. Research has shown that the amount of time an educator waits for a student to answer after posing a question has a critical effect on learning. So, after you ask a student a question, silently count to five (or ten, if you have a student who struggles to get his or her thoughts into words) before giving any additional prompts or redirecting the question to another student.

Bloom's Taxonomy

The questions that follow each passage in *Comprehension and Critical Thinking* assess all levels of learning by following Bloom's Taxonomy, a six-level classification system for comprehension questions that was devised by Benjamin Bloom in 1956. The questions that follow each passage are always presented in order, progressing from *knowledge* to *evaluation*.

The skills listed for each level are essential to keep in mind when teaching comprehension in order to assure that your students reach the higher levels of thinking. Use this classification to form your own questions whenever your students listen to or read material.

Level 1: Knowledge—Students recall information or find requested information in an article. They show memory of dates, events, places, people, and main ideas.

Level 2: Comprehension—Students understand information. This means that they can find information that is stated in a different way from how the question is presented. It also means that students can rephrase or restate information in their own words.

Level 3: Application—Students apply their knowledge to a specific situation. They may be asked to do something new with the knowledge.

Level 4: Analysis—Students break things into components and examine those parts. They notice patterns in information.

Level 5: Synthesis—Students do something new with the information. They pull knowledge together to create new ideas. They generalize, predict, plan, and draw conclusions.

Level 6: Evaluation—Students make judgments and assess value. They form opinions and defend them. They can also understand another person's viewpoint.

Practice Suggestions: Short-Answer Questions

The short-answer question for each passage is evaluative—the highest level of Bloom's Taxonomy. It is basically an opinion statement with no definitive right answer. The students are asked to take stances and defend them. While there is no correct response, it is critical to show the students how to support their opinions using facts and logic. Show the students a format for response—state their opinion followed by the word *because* and a reason. For example, "I do not think that whales should be kept at sea parks because they are wild animals and don't want to be there. They want to be in the ocean with their friends." Do not award credit unless the child adequately supports his or her conclusion. Before passing back the practice papers, make note of two children who had opposing opinions. Then, during the discussion, call on each of these students to read his or her short-answer response to the class. (If all the children drew the same conclusion, come up with support for the opposing one yourself.)

Introduction and Research (cont.)

Practice Suggestions: Document-Based Questions

It is especially important to guide your students in how to understand, interpret, and respond to the document-based questions. For these questions, in order to formulate a response, the students will have to rely on their prior knowledge and common sense in addition to the information provided in the document. Again, the best way to teach this is to demonstrate through thinking aloud how to figure out an answer. Since these questions are usually interpretive, you can allow for some variation in student responses.

The more your students practice, the more competent and confident they will become. Plan to have the class do every exercise in *Comprehension and Critical Thinking*. If you have some students who cannot read the articles independently, allow them to read with partners, and then work through the comprehension questions alone. Eventually, all students must practice reading and answering the questions independently. Move to this stage as soon as possible. For the most effective practice sessions, follow these steps:

1. Have the students read the text silently and answer the questions.

2. Collect all the papers to score the short-answer question and the document-based question portion.

3. Return the papers to their owners, and discuss how the students determined their answers.

4. Refer to the exact wording in the passage.

5. Point out how students had to use their background knowledge to answer certain questions.

6. Discuss how a student should explain his or her stance in each short-answer question.

7. Discuss the document-based question thoroughly.

Scoring the Practice Passages

Identify the number of correct responses when scoring the practice passages. Share the number of correct responses with the students. This is the number they will most easily identify; additionally, the number of correct responses coincides with the Student Achievement Graph. However, for your own records and to share with the parents, you may want to keep track of numeric scores for each student. If you choose to do this, do not write the numeric score on the paper.

To generate a numeric score, follow these guidelines:

Type of Question	Number of Questions	Points Possible Per Question	Total Number of Points
Short-answer question	6	10 points	60 points
Document-based question	2	20 points	40 points
Total			100 points

Standardized Test Success

One of the key objectives of *Comprehension and Critical Thinking* is to prepare your students to get the best possible scores on the reading portion of standardized tests. A student's ability to do well on traditional standardized tests in comprehension requires these factors:

- a large vocabulary
- test-taking skills
- the ability to effectively cope with stress

Every student in your class needs instruction in test-taking skills. Even fluent readers and logical thinkers will perform better on standardized tests if you provide instruction in the following areas:

Understanding the question—Teach the students how to break down the question to figure out what is really being asked. This book will prepare the students for the kinds of questions they will encounter on standardized tests.

Concentrating only on what the text says—Show the students how to restrict their responses to only what is asked. When you review the practice passages, ask your students to show where they found the correct response in the text.

Ruling out distracters in multiple-choice answers—Teach the students to look for the key words in a question and look for those specific words to find the information in the text. They also need to know that they may have to look for synonyms for the key words.

Maintaining concentration—Use classroom time to practice this in advance. Reward the students for maintaining concentration. Explain to them the purpose of this practice and the reason why concentration is so essential.

Teaching Nonfiction Comprehension Skills

Nonfiction comprehension encompasses many skills that develop with a lot of practice. The following information offers a brief overview of the crucial skills of recognizing text structure, visualizing, summarizing, and learning new vocabulary. This information is designed for use with other classroom materials, not the practice passages in *Comprehension and Critical Thinking*.

Many of these skills can be found in scope-and-sequence charts and standards for reading comprehension:

- recognizes the main idea
- identifies details
- determines sequence
- recalls details
- labels parts
- summarizes
- identifies time sequence
- describes character(s)
- retells information in own words

- classifies, sorts into categories
- compares and contrasts
- makes generalizations
- draws conclusions
- recognizes text organization
- predicts outcome and consequences
- experiences an emotional reaction to a text
- recognizes facts
- applies information to a new situation

Typical Comprehension Questions

Teaching the typical kinds of standardized-test questions gives students an anticipation framework and helps them learn how to comprehend what they read. It also boosts their test scores. Questions generally found on standardized reading comprehension tests are as follows:

Facts—questions based on what the text states: who, what, when, where, why, and how

Sequence—questions based on order: what happened first, last, and in-between

Conditions—questions asking the students to compare, contrast, and find the similarities and differences

Summarizing—questions that require the students to restate, paraphrase, choose main ideas, conclude, and select a title

Vocabulary—questions based on word meaning, synonyms and antonyms, proper nouns, words in context, technical words, geographical words, and unusual adjectives

Outcomes—questions that ask readers to draw upon their own experiences or prior knowledge, which means that students must understand cause and effect, consequences, and implications

Opinion—questions that ask the author's intent and require the use of inference skills

Document-based—questions that require students to analyze information from a source document to draw a conclusion or form an opinion

Teaching Nonfiction Comprehension Skills (cont.)

Teaching Text Structure

Students lacking in knowledge of text structure are at a distinct disadvantage, yet this skill is sometimes overlooked in instruction. When referring to a text to locate information to answer a question, understanding structure allows students to quickly locate the right area in which to look. The students also need to understand text structure in order to make predictions and improve overall comprehension.

Some students have been so immersed in print that they have a natural understanding of structure. For instance, they realize that the first sentence of a paragraph often contains the main idea, followed by details about that idea. But many students need direct instruction in text structure. The first step in this process is making certain that students know the way that authors typically present ideas in writing. This knowledge is a major asset for students.

Transitional paragraphs join together two paragraphs to make the writing flow. Most transitional paragraphs do not have a main idea. In all other paragraph types, there is a main idea, even if it is not stated. In the following examples, the main idea is italicized. In order of frequency, the four types of expository paragraph structures are as follows:

1. **The main idea is often the first sentence of a paragraph. The rest of the paragraph provides the supporting details.**

   Clara Barton, known as America's first nurse, was a brave and devoted humanitarian. While caring for others, she was shot at, got frostbitten fingers, and burned her hands. She had severe laryngitis twice and almost lost her eyesight. Yet she continued to care for the sick and injured until she died at the age of 91.

2. **The main idea may fall in the center of the paragraph, surrounded on both sides by details.**

   The coral has created a reef where more than 200 kinds of birds and about 1,500 types of fish live. *In fact, Australia's Great Barrier Reef provides a home for many interesting animals.* These include sea turtles, giant clams, crabs, and crown-of-thorns starfish.

3. **The main idea comes at the end of the paragraph as a summary of the details that came before.**

   Each year, Antarctica spends six months in darkness, from mid-March to mid-September. The continent is covered year-round by ice, which causes sunlight to reflect off its surface. It never really warms up. In fact, the coldest temperature ever recorded was in Antarctica. *Antarctica has one of the harshest environments in the world.*

4. **The main idea is not stated in the paragraph and must be inferred from the details given. This paragraph structure is the most challenging for primary students.**

   The biggest sea horse ever found was over a foot long. Large sea horses live along the coasts of New Zealand, Australia, and California. Smaller sea horses live off the coast of Florida, in the Caribbean Sea, and in the Gulf of Mexico. The smallest adult sea horse ever found was only one-half inch long!

   In this example, the implied main idea is that sea horses' sizes vary based on where they live.

Teaching Nonfiction Comprehension Skills *(cont.)*

Teaching Text Structure *(cont.)*

Some other activities that will help your students understand text structure include the following:

Color code—While reading a text, have the students use different-colored pencils or highlighters to color-code important elements such as the main idea (red), supporting details (yellow), causes (green) and effects (purple), and facts (blue) and opinions (orange). When they have finished, ask them to describe the paragraph's structure in their own words.

Search the text—Teach the students to identify the key words in a question and look specifically for those words in the passage. Then, when you discuss a comprehension question with the students, ask them, "Which words will you look for in the text to find the answer? If you can't find the words, can you find synonyms? Where will you look for the words?"

Signal words—There are specific words used in text that indicate, or signal, that the text has a cause-effect, sequence, or comparison structure. Teaching your students these words will greatly improve their abilities to detect text structure and increase their comprehension.

These Signal Words	Indicate
since, because, caused by, as a result, before and after, so, this led to, if/then, reasons, brought about, so that, when/then, that's why	cause and effect The answer to "Why did it happen?" is a cause. The answer to "What happened?" is an effect.
first, second, third, next, then, after, before, last, later, since then, now, while, meanwhile, at the same time, finally, when, at last, in the end, since that time, following, on (date), at (time)	sequence
but, even if, even though, although, however, instead, not only, unless, yet, on the other hand, either/or, as well as, "–er" and "–st" words (such as better, best, shorter, tallest, bigger, smallest, most, worst)	compare/contrast

Teaching Visualization Skills

Visualization—Visualization is seeing the words of a text as mental images. It is a significant factor that sets proficient readers apart from low-achieving ones. Studies have shown that the ability to generate vivid images while reading strongly correlates with a person's comprehension of text. However, research has also revealed that 20 percent of all children do not visualize or experience sensory images when reading. These children are thus handicapped in their ability to comprehend text, and they are usually the students who avoid and dislike reading because they never connect to text in a personal, meaningful way.

Active visualization can completely engross a reader in text. You have experienced this when you just could not put a book down and you stayed up all night just to finish it. Skilled readers automatically weave their own memories into text as they read to make personalized, lifelike images. In fact, every person develops a unique interpretation of any text. This personalized reading experience explains why most people prefer a book to its movie.

Visualization is not static; unlike photographs, these are "movies in the mind." Mental images must constantly be modified to incorporate new information as it is disclosed by the text. Therefore, your students must learn how to revise their images if they encounter information that requires them to do so.

Sensory Imaging—Sensory imaging employs other senses besides sight, and is closely related to visual imaging. It too has been shown to be crucial to the construction of meaning during reading. This is because the more senses that are employed in a task, the more neural pathways are built, resulting in more avenues to access information. You have experienced sensory imaging when you could almost smell the smoke of a forest fire or taste the sizzling bacon, or laughed along with a character as you read. Sensory imaging connects the reader personally and intimately to the text and breathes life into words.

Since visualization is a challenging skill for one out of every five students to develop, begin with simple fictional passages to scaffold their attempts and promote success. After your students have experienced success with visualization and sensory imaging in literature, they are ready to employ these techniques in nonfiction text.

Visualization has a special significance in nonfiction text. The technical presentation of ideas in nonfiction text coupled with new terms and concepts often overwhelm and discourage students. Using visualization can help students move beyond these barriers. As an added benefit, people who create mental images display better long-term retention of factual material.

Clearly, there are important reasons to teach visualization and sensory imaging skills to students. But perhaps the most compelling reason is this: visualizing demands active involvement, turning passive students into active constructors of meaning.

Teaching Nonfiction Comprehension Skills (cont.)

Teaching Visualization Skills (cont.)

Doing Think-Alouds—It is essential for you to introduce visualization by doing think-alouds to describe your own visualization of text. To do this, read aloud the first one or two lines of a passage and describe what images come to your mind. Be sure to include details that were not stated in the text, such as the house has two stories and green shutters. Then, read the next two lines, and explain how you add to or modify your image based on the new information provided by the text. When you are doing a think-aloud for your class, be sure to do the following:

- Explain how your images help you to better understand the passage.
- Describe details, being sure to include some from your own schema.
- Mention the use of your senses—the more the better.
- Describe your revision of the images as you read further and encounter new information.

Teaching Summarizing

Summarizing informational text is a crucial skill for students to master. It is also one of the most challenging. Summarizing means pulling out only the essential elements of a passage—just the main idea and supporting details. Research has shown that having students put information into their own words causes it to be processed more thoroughly. Thus, summarizing increases both understanding and long-term retention of material. Information can be summarized through such diverse activities as speaking, writing, drawing, or creating a project.

The basic steps of summarizing are as follows:

- Look for the paragraph's main idea sentence; if there is none, create one.
- Find the supporting details, being certain to group all related terms or ideas.
- Record information that is repeated or restated only once.
- Put the summary together into an organized format.

Scaffolding is of critical importance. Your students will need a lot of modeling, guided practice, and small-group or partner practice before attempting to summarize independently. All strategies should be done as a whole group and then with a partner several times before letting the students practice them on their own. Encourage the greatest transfer of knowledge by modeling each strategy's use in multiple content areas.

Teaching Vocabulary

Students may see a word in print that they have never read or heard before. As a result, students need direct instruction in vocabulary to make real progress toward becoming readers who can independently access expository text. Teaching the vocabulary that occurs in a text significantly improves comprehension. Because students encounter vocabulary terms in science, social studies, math, and language arts, strategies for decoding and understanding new words must be taught throughout the day.

Students' vocabularies develop in this order: listening, speaking, reading, and writing. This means that a child understands a word when it is spoken to him or her long before he or she uses it in speech. The child will also understand the word when reading it before attempting to use it in his or her own writing. Each time a child comes across the same word, his or her understanding of that word deepens. Research has shown that vocabulary instruction has the most positive effect on reading comprehension when students encounter the words multiple times. That is why the best vocabulary instruction requires students to use new words in writing and speaking as well as in reading.

Teaching vocabulary can be both effective and fun, especially if you engage the students' multiple modalities (listening, speaking, reading, and writing). In addition, instruction that uses all four modalities is most apt to reach every learner.

The more experience a child has with language, the stronger his or her vocabulary base. Therefore, the majority of vocabulary activities should be done as whole-group or small-group instruction. In this way, children with limited vocabularies can learn from their peers' knowledge bases and will find vocabulary activities less frustrating. Remember, too, that a picture is worth a thousand words. Whenever possible, provide pictures of new vocabulary words.

Selecting Vocabulary Words to Study

Many teachers feel overwhelmed when teaching vocabulary because they realize that it is impossible to thoroughly cover all the words students may not know. Do not attempt to study every unknown word. Instead, choose the words from each selection wisely. Following these guidelines in order will result in an educationally sound vocabulary list:

- Choose words that are critical to the article's meaning.
- Choose conceptually difficult words.
- Choose words with the greatest utility value—those that you anticipate the children will see more often (e.g., choose *horrified* rather than *appalled*).

These suggestions are given for teaching nonfiction material in general. Do not select and preteach vocabulary from these practice passages. You want to simulate real test conditions in which the children would have no prior knowledge of any of the material in any of the passages.

Teaching Vocabulary *(cont.)*

Elements of Effective Vocabulary Instruction

Vocabulary instruction is only effective if students permanently add the concepts to their knowledge bases. Research has shown that the most effective vocabulary program includes contextual, structural, and classification strategies. You can do this by making certain that your vocabulary instruction includes the following elements:

- using context clues
- knowing the meaning of affixes (prefixes, suffixes) and roots
- introducing new words as synonyms and antonyms of known words

Using Context Clues

Learning vocabulary in context is important for two reasons. First, it allows students to become active in determining word meanings; and second, it transfers into their lives by offering them a way to figure out unknown words in their independent reading. If you teach your students how to use context clues, you may eventually be able to omit preteaching any vocabulary that is defined in context (so long as the text is written at your students' independent level).

There are five basic kinds of context clues.

- **Definition**—The definition is given elsewhere in the sentence or paragraph.

  Example: The ragged, *tattered* dress hung from her shoulders.

- **Synonym**—A synonym or synonymous phrase is immediately used in the sentence.

  Example: Although she was overweight, her *obesity* never bothered her until she went to middle school.

- **Contrast**—The meaning may be implied through contrast to a known word or concept. Be alert to these words that signal contrast: *although*, *but*, *however*, and *even though*.

  Example: Although Adesha had always been *prompt*, today he was 20 minutes late.

- **Summary**—The meaning is summed up by a list of attributes.

  Example: Tundra, desert, grassland, and rain forest are four of Earth's *biomes*.

- **Mood**—The meaning of the word can sometimes be grasped from the mood of the larger context in which it appears. The most difficult situation is when the meaning must be inferred with few other clues.

  Example: Her *shrill* voice was actually making my ears hurt.

Teaching Vocabulary (cont.)

Building Vocabulary

Your general approach to building vocabulary should include the following:

Brainstorming—Students brainstorm a list of words associated with a familiar word, sharing everyone's knowledge and thoroughly discussing unfamiliar words.

Semantic mapping—Students sort the brainstormed words into categories, often creating a visual organization tool—such as a graphic organizer or word web—to depict the relationships.

Feature analysis—Students are provided with the key features of the text and a list of terms in a chart, such as a semantic matrix or Venn diagram. Have the students identify the similarities and differences between the items.

Synonyms and antonyms—Introduce both synonyms and antonyms for the words to provide a structure for meaning and substantially and rapidly increase your students' vocabularies.

Analogies—Analogies are similar to synonyms but require higher-level thinking. The goal is to help students identify the relationship between words. Analogies appear on standardized tests in the upper elementary grades.

> **Example:** Bark is to tree as skin is to <u>human</u>.

Word affixes—Studying common prefixes and suffixes helps students deduce new words, especially in context. Teach students to ask, "Does this look like any other word I know? Can I find any word parts I know? Can I figure out the meaning based on its context?"

Important Affixes for Primary Grades

Prefix	Meaning	Example	Suffix	Meaning	Example
un	not	unusual	**-s or -es**	more than one	cars; tomatoes
re	again	redo	**-ed**	did an action	moved
in, im	not	impassable	**-ing**	doing an action	buying
dis	opposite	disassemble	**-ly**	like, very	usually
non	not	nonathletic	**-er**	a person who	farmer
over	too much	overcook	**-ful**	full of	respectful
mis	bad	misrepresent	**-or**	a person who	creator
pre	before	prearrange	**-less**	without	harmless
de	opposite	decompose	**-er**	more	calmer
under	less	underachieve	**-est**	most	happiest

Correlation to Standards

The No Child Left Behind (NCLB) legislation mandates that all states adopt academic standards that identify the skills students will learn in kindergarten through grade 12. While many states had already adopted academic standards prior to NCLB, the legislation set requirements to ensure the standards were detailed and comprehensive.

Standards are designed to focus instruction and guide adoption of curricula. Standards are statements that describe the criteria necessary for students to meet specific academic goals. They define the knowledge, skills, and content students should acquire at each level. Standards are also used to develop standardized tests to evaluate students' academic progress.

In many states today, teachers are required to demonstrate how their lessons meet state standards. State standards are used in the development of Shell Education products, so educators can be assured that they meet the academic requirements of each state.

How to Find Your State Correlations

Shell Education is committed to producing educational materials that are research and standards based. In this effort, all products are correlated to the academic standards of the 50 states, the District of Columbia, and the Department of Defense Dependent Schools. A correlation report customized for your state can be printed directly from the following website: **http://www.shelleducation.com**. If you require assistance in printing correlation reports, please contact Customer Service at 1-877-777-3450.

McREL Compendium

Shell Education uses the Mid-continent Research for Education and Learning (McREL) Compendium to create standards correlations. Each year, McREL analyzes state standards and revises the compendium. By following this procedure, they are able to produce a general compilation of national standards.

Each reading comprehension strategy assessed in this book is based on one or more McREL content standards. The chart below shows the McREL standards that correlate to each lesson used in the book. To see a state-specific correlation, visit the Shell Education website at **http://www.shelleducation.com**.

All lessons in this book are designed to utilize all of the listed standards.

Language Arts Standards

Standard 1 **Uses the general skills and strategies of the writing process.**

   1.2   Uses strategies to draft and revise written work.

Standard 5 **Uses the general skills and strategies of the reading process.**

   5.2   Establishes a purpose for reading.

Standard 7 **Uses reading skills and strategies to understand and interpret a variety of informational texts**.

   7.1   Uses reading skills and strategies to understand a variety of informational texts.

   7.3   Uses text organizers to determine the main idea and to locate information in a text.

   7.5   Summarizes and paraphrases information in texts.

   7.6   Uses prior knowledge and experience to understand and respond to new information.

   7.7   Understands structural patterns or organization in informational texts.

Lights, Animals, Action!

It's 8 A.M. in New York City. Do you know where the gorillas are? Having their morning bananas, of course. The monkeys are waking up just a few doors away. Meanwhile, an elephant is getting a checkup.

Welcome to the Bronx Zoo, the largest city zoo in the United States. The zoo attracts as many as 30,000 people a day. But the place is busy long before any visitors arrive. Zookeepers, veterinarians, a nutritionist, and many others work to keep the animals healthy and happy.

Senior keeper Mark Hoeffling starts his day at 7 A.M. in the kitchen. His cooking is strictly for the birds: a breakfast salad with a side order of worms! Outside, his customers are chirping up a storm. "Morning is a very active time for birds," Hoeffling says.

Over at the Monkey House, keeper Gina Savastano checks to see if any babies were born overnight. Monkeys are full of surprises. "Somebody's always up to something," she says.

Veterinarian Barbara Mangold carries a bag full of medicines on her visits. She never knows who will need her help. "This morning, I worked on an elephant," she said, "and now I'm treating a tiny snake."

The zoo is designed to make the animals feel at home. Jenny Lee helped create the gorillas' rain forest. Now she's working on a home for Siberian tigers. One big challenge: keeping the tigers awake. "We're building big cat toys," she says. Maybe they should put the tigers next to the birds. That noise would keep anyone awake!

Lights, Animals, Action! (cont.)

Directions: Answer these questions. You may look at the article.

1. What is the largest city zoo in the United States?

   _____

   _____

2. Who works to keep the animals healthy and happy?

   _____

   _____

3. Describe some things veterinarian Barbara Mangold might do during her workday.

   _____

   _____

4. In comparing zookeepers, veterinarians, and nutritionists, which job do you think would be the most difficult? Why?

   _____

   _____

5. What could someone say to convince you to work at the zoo?

   _____

   _____

6. What type of big cat toys would you create for the Siberian tigers?

   _____

   _____

7. What would you tell people about the Bronx Zoo to encourage them to visit?

   _____

   _____

Lights, Animals, Action! *(cont.)*

Directions: Look at the recipe below. Answer the questions.

Here is a recipe that the zookeepers at the Bronx Zoo use to feed many of their birds:

Bird Salad

15 quarts chopped mixed vegetables (carrots, beans, peas, corn)

15 quarts diced apples and pears

6 quarts blueberries

2 quarts sliced grapes

8 cups salad supplement (vitamins and minerals)

1. List your three favorite ingredients from Bird Salad.

   _____

   _____

2. What do most of the ingredients have in common?

   _____

   _____

3. Create a recipe that senior keeper Mark Hoeffling might use to feed the gorillas.

   _____

   _____

   _____

   _____

On Top of the World

On May 29, 1953, Edmund Hillary and Tenzing Norgay got a view of Asia that no human had ever enjoyed. They became the first to look down from the top of the world's tallest mountain, Everest. But it wasn't a time for celebrating.

"I didn't leap or throw my hands in the air," Hillary, now 83, told Robert Sullivan of LIFE books. "We were tired, of course." Recently, the party was on! Hillary joined his friends and fans in Nepal. They celebrated the climb's 50th anniversary.

In 1852, Everest was declared the world's tallest mountain. Climbing to the top of the 29,035-foot-tall peak became the goal of people looking for adventure. Since 1920, at least 175 men and women have died climbing Everest. Nearly 1,200 others have reached the summit, or top. Ice, snow, wind, and lack of oxygen are a threat to those who tackle the mountain. Many climbers lose toes, ears, and fingers to frostbite. "You cannot conquer Everest," says Jamling Norgay, Tenzing's son. "Everest will give you a chance to stand on top, and that's it."

Sir Edmund Hillary went on to conquer other goals. He led a team across Antarctica to the South Pole. He climbed more mountains. He also helped bring schools and hospitals to Norgay's people, the Sherpas of Nepal. "That's how I'd like to be remembered," he says. "Not for Everest, but for the work I did with my Sherpa friends."

On Top of the World (cont.)

Directions: Answer these questions. You may look at the article.

1. Who were the first two humans to look down from Everest?

_____

_____

2. Since 1920, how many people have died climbing Everest?

_____

_____

3. How many Everest climbers have gotten the chance to stand on top?

_____

_____

4. What supplies would be useful when climbing a tall mountain?

_____

_____

5. Sir Edmund Hillary said that he would "like to be remembered not for Everest, but for the work I did with my Sherpa friends." Why do you think he said that?

_____

_____

6. Why do you think people decide to climb Everest?

_____

_____

7. Imagine that you are on the top of Everest. Describe what you might be thinking and feeling.

_____

_____

On Top of the World *(cont.)*

Directions: Look at the chart. Answer the questions.

World's Highest Mountains

Mountain	Location	Height
Mt. Everest	Nepal and China	29,035 feet
Mt. Huascaran	Peru	22,205 feet
Mt. McKinley	United States	20,329 feet
Kilimanjaro	Tanzania	19,340 feet
Matterhorn	Switzerland and Italy	14,700 feet
Mt. Erebus	Antarctica	12,448 feet
Mt. Cook	New Zealand	12,254 feet

1. Which mountain is the tallest? Which is the shortest?

   _____

   _____

2. How could the information on the chart be useful to climbers?

   _____

   _____

3. Which mountain would you recommend for climbers? Why?

   _____

   _____

From Page to Film

Ron Weasley, Stuart Little, Shrek: What do they have in common? All are characters in books—and all have made the big leap from the printed page to the big screen!

Hollywood has discovered that popular children's books can make hit movies. *Harry Potter and the Sorcerer's Stone* earned more money than any other film in 2001. Filmmakers have also worked their magic with other books, including Dr. Seuss's *The Cat in the Hat.*

It's not easy turning a book into a movie. Screenwriters have a challenging job. They turn written words and imagined scenes into spoken words and action. Sometimes, they must make a 400-page tale fit into two hours. At other times, the screenwriter expands a short story like *Shrek.* That's one reason the film is never exactly the same as the book. "It has to be different," says author Natalie Babbitt, "or it's not going to work." She wrote *Tuck Everlasting.* The movie has a love story that's not even in the book!

Some people are disappointed when the story is changed. Not Chris Van Allsburg, the author of *Jumanji* and *The Polar Express,* which were also made into movies. "A book is often just the starting point," he says. That's good advice for both filmmakers and readers: Start with the book, and *then* go see the movie!

From Page to Film (cont.)

Directions: Answer these questions. You may look at the article.

1. Who are Ron Weasley, Stuart Little, and Shrek?

   _____

   _____

2. Is it easy to turn a book into a movie?

   _____

   _____

3. Why are films never exactly the same as the book?

   _____

   _____

4. What do you prefer, reading a book first and then seeing the movie or seeing a movie and then reading the book?

   _____

   _____

5. How do you think authors feel about their books being made into movies?

   _____

   _____

6. What would happen if books were never made into movies?

   _____

   _____

7. What book do you think could be a hit movie? Why?

   _____

   _____

From Page to Film (cont.)

Directions: Think about a story you have read. Draw some pictures to show how the story might be shown in a film. Answer the questions.

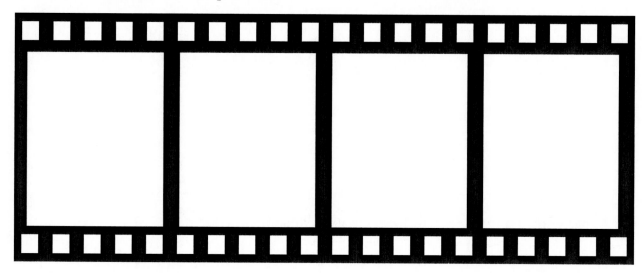

1. What story did you illustrate above?

   _____

   _____

   _____

2. Was it easy or difficult to illustrate the story? Why?

   _____

   _____

   _____

3. How long do you think it would take for you to illustrate a whole story?

   _____

   _____

   _____

A Sister Remembers

Dr. Martin Luther King, Jr. was once a kid, just like you. Now his big sister, Christine King Farris, has written a book about growing up with him. It's called *My Brother Martin*. "I would like kids to know that Martin was a typical boy," Farris says. "If I can get young people to understand that, then they too can make a difference in the world."

Farris and her two brothers grew up in Atlanta, Georgia. Their father was a minister, and their mother was a musician. The King kids loved jokes and pranks. They even fooled neighbors into thinking their grandmother's fur piece was a wild animal! The King children were surrounded by love at home. But the world outside was often cruel and unjust. Their parents tried to shield them from unfair segregation laws that separated black and white people. Farris explains that that's why the family "rarely took streetcars or went to the movies."

When Martin was 7, he asked his mother why people were so mean. Then he told her, "I'm going to turn this world upside down." Farris never forgot her brother's words. As Martin got older, he fought for equality. Farris says there is still work to be done. "We need to continue to make people aware that we're all created equal," she says. Her brother helped change the world. And just like Dr. King, you can, too.

A Sister Remembers (cont.)

Directions: Answer these questions. You may look at the article.

1. What did Christine King Farris write about in her book?

   _____

   _____

2. How did the King kids fool their neighbors?

   _____

   _____

3. Describe a situation when you saw someone being treated unfairly.

   _____

   _____

4. King asked his mother "why people were so mean." How do you think his mother replied? Write three answers she may have given.

   _____

   _____

5. What do you think King meant when he said, "I'm going to turn this world upside down"?

   _____

   _____

6. Write a paragraph about how you can change the world.

   _____

   _____

   _____

   _____

A Sister Remembers (cont.)

Directions: Look at the Persuasive Letter Organizer. Write a letter.

Dr. Martin Luther King, Jr. had a strong opinion about the importance of treating everyone equally. Choose an issue or topic about which you have a strong opinion. Your goal is to convince the reader that your opinion is the correct one. Follow the directions below to help you structure your letter.

_____ **(Your school name)**

_____ **(Your school address)**

_____ **(Today's date)**

_____ **(Greeting)**

Introduction: Describe who you are and why you are writing the letter.

_____

_____

_____

Paragraph 1: Explain the different viewpoints.

_____

_____

_____

Paragraph 2: Describe your viewpoint. Include facts and details to support your opinion.

_____

_____

_____

Paragraph 3: Provide at least two possible solutions to the problem.

_____

_____

_____

Final sentence: Thank the reader for his or her time.

_____

_____ **, (Closing)**

_____ **(Your signature)**

A Nose for the Arts

Boon Yang likes to paint quickly, making long up-and-down streaks in bright colors. Bird prefers to brush deep blue and green across a canvas. People have compared their works to paintings by famous modern artists. But there's a *big* difference: Bird and Boon Yang hold a paintbrush with a trunk!

Boon Yang and Bird are two of about 100 elephants in Thailand and other Asian lands who have become successful artists. Their paintings have sold for as much as $2,200! Some even hang in museums. Painting isn't the only kind of artwork done by Asian elephants. Some are making music too. A Thai elephant orchestra has recorded a CD. The money raised by selling CDs and paintings goes to an elephant-conservation center in Thailand.

Elephants in Thailand are in trouble. For years, they worked carrying heavy logs from rain forests. But the animals lost their jobs in 1989, when Thailand decided to protect the forests and stop logging. Some elephants wound up begging for food! Artists Vitaly Komar and Alex Melamid wanted to help. They set up elephant art schools and brought attention to Thai elephants. Melamid says he's thrilled with the success of the project: "We've shown that anything is possible," he says.

A Nose for the Arts (cont.)

Directions: Answer these questions. You may look at the article.

1. Who are Boon Yang and Bird?

   _____

   _____

2. A Thai elephant orchestra has recorded and sold CDs. What is the money used for?

   _____

   _____

3. Why have some elephants ended up begging for food?

   _____

   _____

4. How did artists Vitaly Komar and Alex Melamid help the elephants?

   _____

   _____

5. How are Boon Yang and Bird's art similar? How is it different?

   _____

   _____

6. Elephants can make art and music. What else do you think they could be taught to do?

   _____

   _____

7. What was something new you learned about elephants after reading the article "A Nose for the Arts?"

   _____

   _____

A Nose for the Arts (cont.)

Directions: Look at the map. Answer the questions.

Below are the approximate population statistics for the Asian elephant.

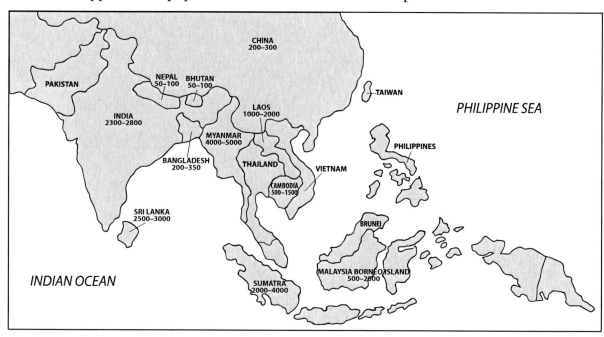

1. How does this map help you understand the article?

   _____

   _____

2. Which country has the largest Asian elephant population?

   _____

   _____

3. Besides the end of logging, what other threats do you think these animals might face?

   _____

   _____

This Croc Rocks

Paul Sereno got quite a shock. A croc shock! The famous paleontologist was digging in the African country of Niger when he found the fossil of a 40-foot-long crocodile. The "supercroc" was as long as a school bus and weighed as much as a small whale!

Don't worry! This giant isn't going to show up in your local pond. Scientists say it last walked the Earth 110 million years ago, long before humans appeared. But the supercroc did have dinosaurs to keep him company—and to eat.

Sereno and his team found the croc bones in October of 2000. They spent a year studying them. They now say that the fossil is the most complete example of a species called *Sarcosuchus imperator* (sar-koh-*soo*-kis im-*peer*-ay-tor). This means *flesh crocodile emperor.*

The king of crocs ruled the African river where it lived. Armorlike bony plates covered parts of its body and protected it from attacks. Its five-foot-long jaw had more than 100 teeth! "This thing could have easily pulled down a good-size dinosaur," Sereno says. The croc's eye sockets were angled so that it could look for prey from underwater. It waited for an animal to stop to get a drink. Then *bam!* It would open its mouth and bite down. "Once one of these clamped onto the leg or neck of an animal," says Sereno, "there wasn't a lot the prey could do."

This Croc Rocks (cont.)

Directions: Answer these questions. You may look at the article.

1. What did Paul Sereno find?

   _____

   _____

2. What did the "supercroc" look like?

   _____

   _____

3. What do you think *imperator* means?

   _____

   _____

4. How did Sereno know that it could eat a dinosaur?

   _____

   _____

5. Why was it so good at spotting prey?

   _____

   _____

6. Why was it so good at protecting itself against attacks?

   _____

   _____

7. Why do you think crocodiles were able to survive into the present day, while dinosaurs were not?

   _____

   _____

This Croc Rocks (cont.)

Directions: Look at the picture. Answer the questions.

Among the very largest crocs to ever live, *Sarcosuchus imperator,* nicknamed Supercroc, stretched out to reach as long as 40 feet and weighed about ten times as much as today's croc.

Supercroc's skull alone measured about six feet—longer than many humans are tall.

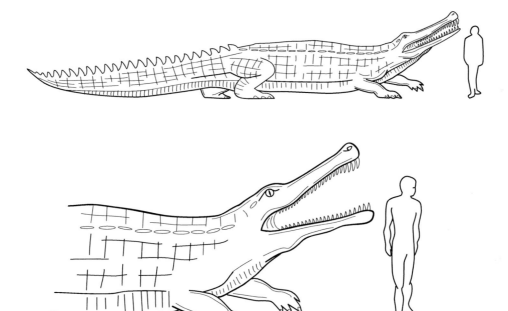

1. How do the illustrations help you understand the article?

   _____

   _____

2. Why do you think the illustrator used a human to compare to the croc?

   _____

   _____

3. What else could the illustrator have used to compare the croc to?

   _____

   _____

Hooray for School

Yakubu, a 14-year-old in Ghana, is pretty old to be in fourth grade. But she's happy just to be in school. Years ago, she had to drop out after the first grade. Her parents were too poor to take care of her. "I had to go to work in a snack bar," she explains. "I cried every day."

There are thousands of girls like Yakubu in Ghana. Boys are more likely to get paying jobs when they get older, so parents send them to school. But now, Campaign for Female Education (CamFed) is giving girls a chance to learn.

CamFed's solution is simple. "It only costs $45 per student per year to go to school," says Ann Cotton, who runs CamFed. The $45 covers school uniforms, books, and other supplies. "We pay for everything until they finish high school." CamFed gets its money from big companies. Nearly all the girls whom it supports finish high school.

Mariama Mohammed works with villagers near Tamale. She asks them to send girls to school. Most of them agree, once they get money to help. She says, "People are starting to realize that if women are educated, the entire society benefits."

Hooray for School (cont.)

Directions: Answer these questions. You may look at the article.

1. Why is Yakubu only in fourth grade?

   _____

   _____

2. Why did she have to drop out of school?

   _____

   _____

3. Why do boys go to school and many girls do not?

   _____

   _____

4. What does CamFed stand for? What does the organization do?

   _____

   _____

5. Why do poor families in the United States still send their children to school?

   _____

   _____

6. How does it benefit society for all children to attend school?

   _____

   _____

Hooray for School *(cont.)*

Directions: Look at the diagram. Answer the questions.

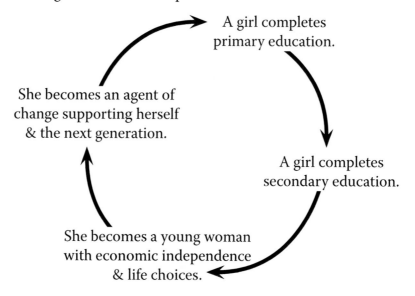

1. How does this diagram help you to understand the article?

   _____

   _____

2. What is the starting point of the cycle?

   _____

   _____

3. Why do you think girls who start primary school would complete their secondary education?

   _____

   _____

4. Why do you think that the diagram is in the shape of a circle?

   _____

   _____

Searching the Heavens

When did the universe begin? Does it stretch on forever? Is there life on distant planets?

Humans have been asking questions like these since they first gazed up at the sky. The answers might be found on mountaintops, where scientists have been building powerful new telescopes. Around the world, from Hawaii to South America to Europe, these superscopes are helping us see farther into space than ever before.

A telescope's power depends largely on the size of the mirror inside it. The bigger the mirror, the more starlight it can catch. A huge, perfect mirror can capture even the faintest star glow.

The new telescopes reflect improvements in how telescope mirrors are built. Older telescopes had thick, heavy mirrors, but there were limits to how big they could be. Some new scopes have thin, flexible mirrors controlled by computers. Others, like the Keck telescope in Hawaii, have jumbo mirrors made up of many small ones. Its mirror is 33 feet across. The Keck is one of four huge new telescopes in Hawaii.

Giant telescopes are helping scientists make amazing discoveries. Astronomer Geoff Marcy has discovered 35 planets circling sunlike stars. "The vast majority of them have been found with Keck," he says. A new telescope in Chile has helped European scientists estimate the age of the universe: 14 billion years.

Astronomers like George Djorgovski in Boston hope to explore the heavens with even bigger telescopes. "We'll almost certainly find things we never could have imagined," he says.

Searching the Heavens (cont.)

Directions: Answer these questions. You may look at the article.

1. What determines a telescope's power?

   _____

   _____

2. How are newer telescopes better than older ones?

   _____

   _____

3. Why do you think scientists chose to place these powerful telescopes on mountaintops?

   _____

   _____

4. What is unique about the Keck telescope, and where is it located?

   _____

   _____

5. What amazing discovery was made with a new telescope in Chile?

   _____

   _____

6. What did Geoff Marcy discover?

   _____

   _____

7. Why do you think it's important to find out more about our universe?

   _____

   _____

Searching the Heavens *(cont.)*

Directions: Look at the diagram. Answer the questions.

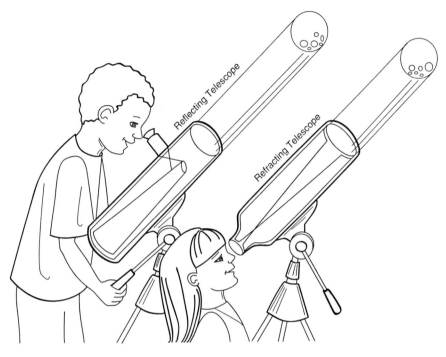

1. How many types of telescopes are shown in the picture?

   _____

   _____

2. Which type of telescope is described in the article? How can you tell?

   _____

   _____

3. If you were going to buy a telescope, which kind would you get? Why?

   _____

   _____

4. How does the diagram help you to understand how a telescope works?

   _____

   _____

The Bully Battle

Christian Champ was in kindergarten the first time he met a bully. A second-grader pushed Christian off a swing. Christian, who lives in Prescott, Arizona, is in fifth grade now. And he knows how to handle bullies. "First I ignore the bully," he says. "Then I tell the teacher."

No one likes to be pushed or teased. Sadly, that's what happens to lots of kids every day. The National Association of School Psychologists says that 5 million kids are bullied each year. About 160,000 kids skip school each day because they're afraid of bullies.

Communities are helping kids. In October, 36 states observed Safe Communities = Safe Schools Awareness Week. Schools held activities to teach kids not to hit or tease.

Rebecca Sassoon, of New York City, knows that words can hurt. When she was 7, she was bullied by three boys. "I got things right on tests, so they teased me," she remembers. "I would cry after school."

Some schools have yearlong antibullying programs. In Massachusetts, lessons start in kindergarten. In Suffern, New York, students promise to show respect every day. Will these new programs really stop the teasing and fighting? There's hope. Bullies can learn to change their ways, says 10-year-old Spencer from Colorado. "I teased people when I was in second grade," Spencer says, "but by third grade, I stopped. I didn't like making people feel bad."

The Bully Battle *(cont.)*

Directions: Answer these questions. You may look at the article.

1. About how many kids are bullied every year?

   _____

   _____

2. Why do you think so many kids are bullies?

   _____

   _____

. 3. How does Christian Champ handle bullies now?

   _____

   _____

4. Why did Rebecca Sassoon get bullied?

   _____

   _____

5. Describe an activity that you think might be included during Safe Communities = Safe Schools Awareness Week.

   _____

   _____

6. When do you think antibullying programs should begin?

   _____

   _____

7. Why is it wrong to bully or tease other people?

   _____

The Bully Battle *(cont.)*

Directions: Read the list. Answer the questions.

What Should You Do if a Bully Bothers You?

1. Tell your parents. Telling is not tattling.
2. If the bullying happened at school, tell a trusted teacher, counselor, or principal, or have your parents talk to someone at the school.
3. Do not retaliate or get angry.
4. Respond evenly and firmly, or say nothing and walk away.
5. Develop friendships and stick up for one another.
6. Act confident.
7. Take a different route to and from school.
8. Avoid unsupervised areas of school.
9. Do not bring expensive items to school.

---

1. Describe a time when you were bullied or you saw someone else bullied.

   _____

   _____

2. How do you think these tips might have helped you or the person you saw bullied? Explain your answer.

   _____

   _____

3. Which do you think is the most valuable tip? Explain your answer.

   _____

   _____

4. Which do you think is the least valuable tip? Explain your answer.

   _____

   _____

Can Venice Be Saved?

No city on Earth can match beautiful Venice, Italy. Built on 118 islands, it is a place where canals serve as streets and boats serve as taxis. Each year, 10 million tourists come to see its gorgeous buildings and artwork. But one of the very things that make Venice special—its waterways—threatens the city.

Venice is sinking! The city was built on marshy land in a lagoon. Over the years, the buildings have been sinking. Meanwhile, climate changes have caused the nearby Adriatic Sea to rise. Seawater often floods the city.

Each year, from October to March, strong winds and high tides cause terrible floods. The worst flooding anyone can remember was on November 4, 1966. Six feet of water destroyed homes and forced businesses to close. The seawater has damaged art treasures and historic sites. Some experts say Venice will sink eight inches in the next 50 years. Already, many citizens are leaving the city.

A group that wants to save Venice has come up with a $2 billion plan to stop the flooding. The plan is called Project Moses. The group wants to place huge underwater gates at the three entrances to the Venice lagoon. The gates would act as dams and hold back the seawater.

Project Moses has been in the works for 10 years. But not everyone likes the idea. Critics argue that by shutting out seawater, the gates would harm the lagoon's fish and plant life.

The Italian government has decided to keep studying the project. That was great news for Maria Teresa Brotto, an engineer who worked on the plan. "People want this problem resolved," she says.

Can Venice Be Saved? *(cont.)*

Directions: Answer these questions. You may look at the article.

1. What is causing the flooding in Venice?

   _____

   _____

2. Why do so many tourists visit?

   _____

   _____

3. What kind of damage has the flooding caused?

   _____

   _____

4. What are the predictions for the city's future?

   _____

   _____

5. What is Project Moses?

   _____

   _____

6. How does the group want to stop the flooding?

   _____

   _____

7. Why don't critics like the idea?

   _____

   _____

Can Venice Be Saved? *(cont.)*

Directions: Look at the map. Answer the questions.

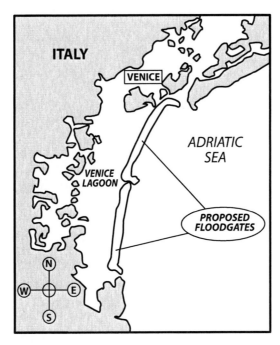

Project Moses: when the Adriatic Sea rises very high, floodgates would inflate and lift up from the ocean floor. They'd keep seawater out of the lagoon and stop flooding in Venice.

1. How many floodgate locations are proposed?

    _____

    _____

2. Where would the water flow after the floodgates are activated?

    _____

    _____

3. What do you think is more important: saving Venice from floods or protecting the lagoon's fish and plant life? Explain your answer.

    _____

    _____

Proud to Be Mohawk

The kids at the Akwesasne Freedom School in Rooseveltown, New York, start their day the same way lots of kids do—chatting about the latest cartoon or Nintendo. But when classes begin, their day takes on a different sound.

The children are learning Kanien'kehá:ka (gah-nyah-gay-*ha*-gah). It is the language of their American Indian ancestors, the Mohawk Indians. "I'm glad I'm learning it," says a third-grader named Kwe:kon (*gweh*-go). "Our people are Mohawk. We should learn it!"

The Freedom School is on the United States side of the St. Regis Reservation, which also has land in Canada. A reservation is an area that has been set aside for American Indians. Hundreds of years ago, American Indians lost much of their land to European settlers and the government. In the 1800s, the government created reservations as places for American Indians to live. Parents started the Freedom School for preschoolers through eighth-graders in 1979. They wanted their children to learn the Mohawk language. Like many American Indian languages, Mohawk was disappearing.

Students at the school also study Mohawk traditions. They sing old Mohawk songs and learn dances. They use native names. "Mine means She Sways with the Grass," says fourth-grader Kahéntawaks (gah-*hon*-dah-walks). Most importantly, the students are learning what it means to be American Indian. Says a teacher, "They're taught to be proud of who they are."

Proud to Be Mohawk (cont.)

Directions: Answer these questions. You may look at the article.

1. Where is the Akwesasne Freedom School, and who started it?

   _____

   _____

2. What is Kanien'kehá:ka?

   _____

   _____

3. What do the children at the school think about learning their native language?

   _____

   _____

4. What is a reservation?

   _____

   _____

5. Why did parents start the school?

   _____

   _____

6. What else do the kids learn besides the language?

   _____

   _____

7. Create a Mohawk name that you would like to have and explain its translation.

   _____

   _____

Proud to Be Mohawk (cont.)

Directions: Look at the list of words. Answer the questions.

Speak Mohawk	The Mohawk Alphabet
Would you like to help save the Mohawk language? Here are some words to get you started: • hello—shé:kon (say-go) • hi—kwe kwe (gweh gweh) • bye—ó:nen (oh-nah) • mom—ista (ee-stah) • dad—rákeni (la-geh-nee) • friend—ó:ri (oh-lee)	The Mohawk alphabet is much shorter than the English alphabet. The combination of certain letters makes different phonetic sounds; for example, **wh** sounds like *f* and **tsi** sounds like *j*. **Vowels** A = short *a* as in *apple* E = *e* as in *get* I = *ē* as in *me* O = *ō* as in *go* **Consonants** T = *d* as in *door* K = *g* as in *good* R = *l* as in *look* S = *z* as in *zoo*

1. Do you think the Mohawk alphabet or the English alphabet is easier to learn? Why?

   _____

   _____

2. What do you think would be the hardest part about learning the Mohawk language?

   _____

   _____

3. Why do you think the alphabet and a list of common words were both included? Which list was more helpful in your understanding of the language?

   _____

   _____

The Latest Lingo

Do you Google in the snain? Not all of these words can be found in *Merriam-Webster's Collegiate Dictionary. Snain,* meaning *a mix of snow and rain,* never caught on. *Google,* meaning "to search the Internet," was added in 2006.

Some 1,000 new words or usages enter the English language each year. Some go into the dictionary. Others fade from use. "Our language is a living thing," says Jim Lowe, an editor at Merriam-Webster. "It keeps growing."

Merriam-Webster first published the *Collegiate Dictionary* in 1898. Since then, at least 100,000 words have been added. As the world changes, we need new words to describe it. The dictionary's editors look in everything from catalogs to comic books for the latest lingo. New words go on index cards that note when and where they first appeared. Lowe reviews these words for the edition's annual updates. Every ten years, the dictionary gets a total makeover. Lowe and the other editors review the one million or so new terms they have found. About 10,000 make it in. For a word to be added, it must show up regularly in a lot of places.

Lowe is no longer surprised by the words he finds. "When I first saw *spam,* I thought it was unusual," he says. "It's hard to associate meats with e-mail." But there it is on page 1,195, in black and white.

The Latest Lingo (cont.)

Directions: Answer these questions. You may look at the article.

1. What does "Do you Google in the snain?" mean?

   _____

2. What did Lowe compare the English language to?

   _____

   _____

3. Why does the dictionary need to be updated?

   _____

   _____

4. How often does the dictionary get updated?

   _____

   _____

5. How often does the dictionary get a complete makeover? How many new terms are usually added?

   _____

   _____

   _____

6. Name two places the dictionary's editors look for new words.

   _____

   _____

7. What are two meanings for *spam*?

   _____

   _____

The Latest Lingo (cont.)

Directions: Read the list of words below. Answer the questions.

Creating Their Own Words

Merriam-Webster's online *Open Dictionary* is a way for word-lovers all over the world to submit words they haven't seen in the dictionary. It provides an often amusing look at the latest words and phrases catching the attention of the online community. Here are some recent submissions:

festivate (verb): combination of celebrate and festival; to create a joyous occasion with friends; to have a good time

"After the final exam, the students decided to *festivate*."

radsome (adjective): radical + awesome = radsome

"Emily, that shirt is *radsome*."

websterling (noun): words that hope to be in Webster's dictionary someday

"The current crop of *websterlings* caused heated debate among the editors at Merriam-Webster."

wog (noun): The activity of walking and jogging alternatively for a period of time.

"A *wog* in the morning is good physical activity."

doggage (noun): a dog that is carried like or handled like baggage

"That celebrity's dog is *doggage*. Have you ever seen its legs touch the ground?"

ignoy (verb): to annoy by ignoring

"Stop *ignoying* me!"

---

1. Which of these words do you think has the best chance of getting into the dictionary? Why?

   _____

   _____

2. Come up with your own idea for a new word and write a letter to the editors at Merriam-Webster, explaining why your word should be a new entry in the dictionary.

   _____

   _____

   _____

   _____

Time for a Checkup?

The tooth fairy might be working overtime this year. According to the largest government dental study in 25 years, tooth decay in baby teeth has risen from 24 percent to 28 percent in children ages 2 to 5 since 1999. Before that, tooth decay had been on the decline for 40 years.

Experts believe that this new trend might have something to do with kids' eating habits. "Parents are giving their children more processed snack foods than in the past, and more bottled water or other drinks instead of fluoridated tap water," said Dr. Bruce Dye of the National Center for Health Statistics, who lead the study.

Bottled water often does not have the right amount of fluoride. Fluoride is a substance that is found naturally in water. Research has shown that at certain levels, it strengthens tooth enamel and helps prevent tooth decay. Many communities add fluoride to their water supplies to tap into this cavity-fighting power. Processed snack foods tend to be loaded with sugar. Sweet, starchy foods stick to the teeth, forming a film. If that film is not brushed away, it can lead to tooth decay.

Thankfully, not all the news is bad. The study found that kids age six to 11 have fewer cavities. Experts think this might be due to the fact that more dentists are using dental sealants, or plastic coatings that are applied to teeth to prevent decay. Adults can also share in the good news. A serious form of gum disease called periodontitis has decreased by 50 percent in adults 20 to 64 years old. "Overall, we can say that most Americans are noticing an improvement in their oral health," Dye said.

Time for a Checkup? *(cont.)*

Directions: Answer these questions. You may look at the article.

1. What do you think the first sentence about the "tooth fairy...working overtime" is supposed to mean?

   _____

   _____

2. What has happened to tooth-decay rates in baby teeth since 1999? Why did this surprise researchers?

   _____

   _____

3. What do experts blame for the tooth decay problem in young children?

   _____

   _____

4. How is bottled water part of the problem?

   _____

   _____

5. What is the good news for adults?

   _____

   _____

6. Do you think your own dental health has improved or worsened over the past five years? What do you think the reasons are behind the change?

   _____

   _____

Time for a Checkup? *(cont.)*

Directions: Look at the diagram of the tooth. Answer the questions.

Tooth Anatomy

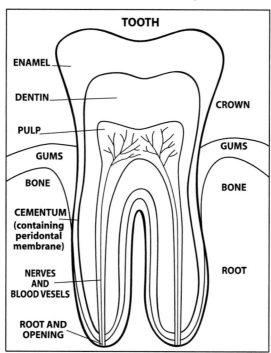

1. Which part of the tooth does fluoride strengthen?

   _____

   _____

2. What is the visible part of the tooth called?

   _____

   _____

3. Which parts of the tooth are located below the gum line? Which part do you think is responsible for the pain you feel when you have a toothache? Why do you think that?

   _____

   _____

Cities of Tomorrow

In the African city of Mwinda, floating farms are quite common. The city's residents zip around in hydrogen-powered hover vehicles. Renewable energy resources provide the city's power. That's how Jake Bowers and Krisha Sherburne, both 12, and Emily Ponti, 14, envisioned their future city.

The students attend St. Thomas More School in Baton Rouge, Louisiana. They took first place for their design in the 2007 National Engineer Week Future City Competition held in Washington, D.C. The students won a trip to the United States Space Camp in Huntsville, Alabama.

Kids from 35 middle schools across the country made it to Washington. They had teamed up with teachers and volunteer engineer mentors to develop cities. Each team began by creating a fictional city on *SimCity 3000*. The computer game allows players to construct towns. The students then built a tabletop model of the city. They wrote an essay and presented their creation to a panel of judges. This year's theme asked students to design fuel cell-powered communities. Fuel-cell technology works by using hydrogen and oxygen to produce power. The process is environmentally friendly.

Organizers hope the contest provides a fun and educational way to spark young people's interest in engineering. "As the number of graduates in engineering [decreases], it's even more important to encourage students to build these skills at an early age," says John Hofmeister, president of Shell Oil Company. Shell is a sponsor of the annual Future City contest.

Plenty of kids seem to be getting the message. Some 30,000 students from more than 1,000 schools participated in the 2006–2007 Future City Competition.

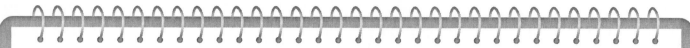

Cities of Tomorrow (cont.)

Directions: Answer these questions. You may look at the article.

1. Describe the city that Jake Bowers, Krisha Sherburne, and Emily Ponti designed. Include the city's name and location.

   _____

   _____

2. What did all the cities in this competition have in common?

   _____

   _____

3. Why do you think the contest was held in Washington, D.C.?

   _____

   _____

4. What was the first step for the teams when they were designing their cities?

   _____

   _____

5. What was the final step in the process?

   _____

   _____

6. Why do you think students were asked to design an environmentally friendly city?

   _____

   _____

Cities of Tomorrow (cont.)

Directions: Look at the list. Answer the questions.

Design Your Own City

Roads	Water	Library
Police Department	Parks	Garbage Pickup
Hospital	City Hall	Zoo
Transportation	Power	Landfill
Fire Department Schools	Playgrounds	

1. If you were designing a new city, which five items from this list would you have as your top priorities? Why would you choose those as the most important parts of your city?

   _____

   _____

   _____

2. Which two things from the list do you think are least important for a city to spend money on? Explain your answer.

   _____

   _____

   _____

3. Does the city you live in now have a lot of traffic? Crowded schools? A library that's too small? From the list above, choose three things that you wish the city you live in now would make a higher priority. Explain what you would like your city leaders to do to fix these problems.

   _____

   _____

   _____

Play Ball!

Major-league baseball hit a home run when it opened the Urban Youth Academy in Compton, California last spring. Organizers hoped the academy, the first of its kind, would be a positive force in the community. But most of all, they wanted to get kids excited about America's pastime.

The academy is the vision of baseball executive Jimmy Lee Solomon. He says his goal was to bring a lush, green playing field to inner-city kids. Kids ages seven to 17 can participate for free at the year-round school. Former major leaguers head the six-week-long after-school instructional camps. Last month, Hall of Famer Rod Carew stopped by to share hitting tips.

Are kids loving it? Ask Priscilla Mota, 10, who plays softball at the academy. Although she was on Little League teams, she says that they did not offer "many opportunities to learn [hitting and catching]." She likes that the academy has taught her a wide variety of skills.

Academy director Darrell Miller is a former catcher for the Los Angeles Angels of Anaheim. He tells future big-leaguers that schoolwork is just as important as baseball. The academy offers tutoring as well as college-prep classes for high school students. "As we're growing, it's becoming evident that the community is hungry for what we've got to offer," Miller says.

Play Ball! *(cont.)*

Directions: Answer these questions. You may look at the article.

1. Why did organizers want to start this camp?

   _____

   _____

2. Who teaches baseball to the kids? Why do you think they volunteer to teach baseball to inner-city kids?

   _____

   _____

3. Do you think many of the kids who go to this camp have had a chance to go to a major-league baseball game? Why or why not?

   _____

   _____

4. Why do you think schoolwork is emphasized at the camp, too?

   _____

   _____

5. Would you want to go to a camp like this one? Why or why not?

   _____

   _____

6. Do you think it's fair that inner-city kids get to go to a camp like this for free, when it might cost hundreds of dollars for someone else? Explain your answer.

   _____

   _____

Play Ball! *(cont.)*

Directions: Look at the diagram. Answer the questions.

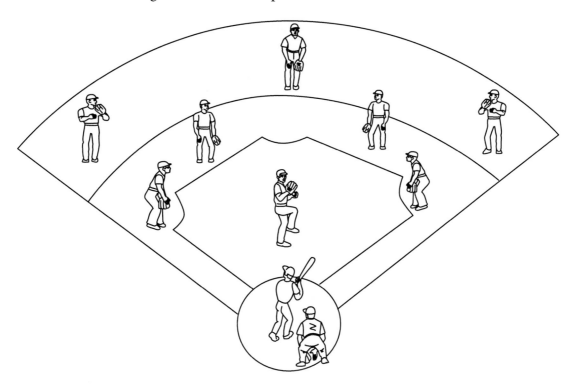

1. How is this diagram related to the article?

   _____

   _____

2. How many players are needed on one team for a regulation game of baseball?

   _____

   _____

3. One of the most important parts of being an athlete is having a coach who helps you become better at your sport. What do you think makes a great coach? What do you think coaches should care about most? Explain your answer.

   _____

   _____

On the Money

Hundreds of people lined up at Grand Central Terminal recently, but they weren't there to catch a train. They came to New York City's famous railroad station to trade in old dollar bills for the new George Washington presidential $1 coin.

The gold-colored coin is the first in a new series by the United States Mint that honors former presidents. The Mint will issue four presidential $1 coins a year through 2016. Like the popular 50-state quarters program, which issues coins in the order in which each state joined the Union, presidential $1 coins will come out in the order in which each president served. The George Washington coin is the first to be released. The John Adams, Thomas Jefferson, and James Madison coins are next.

Each coin will show a different president on its face, or heads side. It will also show the president's name, the order in which he served, and his years in office. The other side of the coin will show the Statue of Liberty and the inscriptions *United States of America* and *$1*.

The coins aren't just for collectors. "The new presidential $1 coins are an educational and fun way to learn about former presidents," says United States Mint director Edmund Moy. They have practical uses, too. At Grand Central Terminal, Moy kicked off the coin exchange by placing a presidential $1 coin in a New York City parking meter.

On the Money (cont.)

Directions: Answer these questions. You may look at the article.

1. What popular coin program does the article compare the Presidential $1 Coin Program to?

   _____

   _____

2. In what order will the presidential coins be issued?

   _____

   _____

3. Why do you think that the director of the United States Mint put the coin in a parking meter at the ceremony for the new coin?

   _____

   _____

4. Why do you think the United States Mint is releasing just four coins each year instead of releasing them all at once?

   _____

   _____

5. Why do you think people don't use $1 coins as much as they use dollar bills?

   _____

   _____

6. Would you want to collect presidential $1 coins? Why or why not?

   _____

   _____

On the Money (cont.)

Directions: Look at the pictures and read the descriptions. Answer the questions.

Circulating Dollar Coins

The Presidential $1 Coin Program began with our first president, George Washington, and continues with each president in order of service, bringing out four new designs every year.

The Golden Dollar shows Sacagawea, the young Shoshone Indian woman who helped Lewis and Clark explore the territory called Louisiana. The baby she carries on her back was born during the expedition.

The Susan B. Anthony Dollar was produced from 1979–1981. Susan B. Anthony's (1820–1906) brave fight to get women the right to vote earned her a place on the dollar coin. She is known as a founder of the women's suffrage movement.

1. What are three similarities that these coins share?

   _____

   _____

2. What are three differences?

   _____

   _____

3. It has been hard for the United States Mint to get people to use $1 coins. Do you think the Presidential $1 Coin Program will be more successful than other $1 coins? Explain your answer.

   _____

   _____

A Subway Superhero

Wesley Autrey can't fly, but he is still being called a real-life Superman! The brave 50-year-old recently rescued Cameron Hollopeter from being hit by a train. The train was entering a subway station in New York City. The young man had fallen from the station's platform and onto the train tracks a few feet below.

Autrey, a construction worker and Navy veteran, was with his two young daughters when he saw Hollopeter fall. Autrey made a quick decision and jumped onto the tracks. He then rolled himself and Hollopeter into a gap, or opening, between the rails. Autrey used his own body to shield the young man.

Five of the train's cars passed over the two before stopping. The two men were both unhurt. Hollopeter's stepmother, Rachel Hollopeter, called Autrey an angel. For his bravery, Autrey was given a hero's welcome at City Hall. The New York City mayor presented Autrey with the Bronze Medallion. It is the city's highest award for achievements by its citizens. Mayor Bloomberg called Autrey "a great man—a man who makes us all proud to be New Yorkers."

After the ceremony at City Hall, a limousine took Autrey to a meeting with multimillionaire businessman Donald Trump. Trump rewarded Autrey with $10,000. The heroic father also received a trip to Disney World and one year of free subway rides.

Even after all this attention, Autrey still doesn't see himself as a Superman. "I did it out of a split-second reaction," Autrey said. "And if I had to do it again, I probably would."

A Subway Superhero (cont.)

Directions: Answer these questions. You may look at the article.

1. Why would Autrey be compared to Superman?

   _____

   _____

2. What would probably have happened if Autrey had not made the decision to jump down to the tracks?

   _____

   _____

3. How do you think Autrey's young daughters must have felt when they saw their father jump down onto the train tracks?

   _____

   _____

4. What kinds of awards and gifts did Autrey receive for his heroic act?

   _____

   _____

5. Autrey called his decision to jump a "split-second reaction." If you were in a similar situation, what do you think you would have done? Why?

   _____

   _____

6. Being a hero doesn't only mean saving someone's life. Helping an elderly person around the house or helping a sibling with homework can make you a hero, too. Describe a time when someone may have thought of you as a hero.

   _____

   _____

A Subway Superhero (cont.)

Directions: Read the list. Answer the questions.

What Makes a Hero?

1. A hero is brave.

2. A hero is dishonest.

3. A hero is always a popular person.

4. A hero thinks of others before himself or herself.

5. A hero is never scared.

6. A hero is always a celebrity.

7. A hero isn't afraid to stand up for himself or herself.

8. A hero always wants to be rewarded for his or her actions.

9. A hero is always physically strong.

10. A hero is thoughtful.

---

1. List the numbered statements that you think are true.

   _____

   _____

2. List the numbered statements that you think are false.

   _____

   _____

3. What other characteristics would you use to describe a hero?

   _____

   _____

4. Write about someone you consider a hero. Describe what makes that person a hero to you.

   _____

   _____

This Panda Is a Beauty

The youngest giant panda cub in the United States was recently named. Mei Lan, which means *Atlanta Beauty*, was the top vote-getter in an online poll sponsored by the Atlanta Zoo in Georgia. When she was born, Mei Lan weighed about 4 ounces. Now Mei Lan weighs about 12 pounds and is 26.5 inches long! She is the fifth giant panda born at a United States zoo in the last six years.

Just recently, Mei Lan stood up on her own. She should be walking soon. Soon after Mei Lan takes her first steps, the public will be able to meet her. Until then, Mei Lan and her mother, Lun Lun, can be seen on the zoo's online panda-cam or through a live video feed shown on monitors at the zoo's panda habitat. The father, Yang Yang, is being kept apart from mother and baby. That is normal when a giant panda cub is so young.

Giant pandas are an endangered species. There are only 1,600 to 3,000 remaining in the wild today. Most pandas in the wild live in the mountains. There, they are safe from development that threatens their habitat. Another 185 pandas live in captivity, mostly in China. The only other United States zoos that have pandas are in San Diego, Memphis, and Washington, D.C.

This Panda Is a Beauty (cont.)

Directions: Answer these questions. You may look at the article.

1. Why is the birth of a giant panda at a United States zoo so important?

   _____

   _____

2. How was the panda's name selected?

   _____

   _____

3. Why do you think that name was chosen?

   _____

   _____

4. Why do you think the father might be separated from the mother and baby?

   _____

   _____

5. Why do you think most giant pandas live in the mountains?

   _____

   _____

6. Where do most pandas live in captivity? Why do you think that is?

   _____

   _____

7. Why do you think so many people come to see giant pandas at United States zoos?

   _____

   _____

This Panda Is a Beauty (cont.)

Directions: Look at the chart. Answer the questions.

The World's Eight Bear Species

Common Name	Habitat	Diet	Status	Continent
giant panda	bamboo forest	herbivore	endangered	Asia
sun bear	tropical rainforest	omnivore	endangered	Asia
sloth bear	tropical rainforest	omnivore	vulnerable	Asia
Asiatic black bear	temperate forest	omnivore	vulnerable	Asia
American black bear	temperate forest	omnivore	common	North America
spectacled bear	mountains	omnivore	vulnerable	South America
brown bear	varied	omnivore	threatened	North America, Eurasia
polar bear	polar ice	carnivore	potentially threatened	North America, Eurasia

1. *Omnipotent* means having power over all. *Omnipresent* means present in all places at all times. *Omniscient* means knowing all. A sun bear is an *omnivore*. What do you think it eats?

   _____

   _____

2. Which one of the eight types of bears do you think is least likely to become extinct? Why?

   _____

   _____

3. The survival of the rainforest is in danger. Global warming is threatening polar ice. How might that affect the bear population? Explain your answer.

   _____

   _____

Looks a Lot Like Earth

Is there life beyond planet Earth? For the first time, astronomers have discovered a planet outside our solar system that could sustain life. It was discovered by the European Southern Observatory's telescope located in Chile. "It's a significant step on the way to finding possible life in the universe," says Michel Mayor. He is one of the 11 European astronomers on the team that discovered the planet.

Astronomers have already identified Mars as a possible site of alien life. But until now, all 220 planets that astronomers have found outside our solar system have had what they describe as the Goldilocks problem: they have either been too hot or too cold to sustain life. The newfound planet, named 581 c, could be just right.

The new planet has Earthlike temperatures and is about five times heavier than Earth. Because its gravity is stronger, a 150-pound person on Earth would feel like 240 pounds on 581 c. Astronomers need to learn a lot more about the planet. One of the most important questions is: Does it have water? "Liquid water is critical to life as we know it," says Xavier Delfosse, an astronomer on the discovery team.

The planet is the right temperature for liquid water, but there is not yet any evidence of its existence.

The planet is located 120 trillion miles, or 20.5 light years, away from Earth. While the distance will make it impossible to study the planet in person, it won't stop scientists from searching for signs of life. "This planet will most probably be a very important target of the future space missions dedicated to the search for extraterrestrial life," says Delfosse. "On the treasure map of the universe, one would be tempted to mark this planet with an X."

Name _____

Looks a Lot Like Earth (cont.)

Directions: Answer these questions. You may look at the article.

1. Why is finding 581 c big news?

   _____

   _____

2. The force that pulls you to Earth determines your weight. What is that force called?

   _____

   _____

3. The article says that water is critical to life. Why is that?

   _____

   _____

4. Before now, planets have either been too hot or too cold to sustain life. Planet 581 c may be just right. Why is this called the "Goldilocks problem"?

   _____

   _____

5. Why does the distance make it impossible to study the planet in person?

   _____

   _____

6. What does it mean on the treasure map when you mark something with an X?

   _____

   _____

7. Do you believe there is life on other planets? Why or why not?

   _____

   _____

Looks a Lot Like Earth (cont.)

Directions: Read the information below. Answer the questions.

How Did the Planets Get Their Names?

All of the planets, except for Earth, were named after Greek and Roman gods and goddesses. Jupiter, Saturn, Mars, Venus, and Mercury were given their names thousands of years ago. The other planets were not discovered until much later, when telescopes were invented. The tradition of naming the planets after Greek and Roman gods and goddesses was carried on for the last three planets discovered as well.

- Mercury was named after the Roman god of travel.

- Venus was the Roman goddess of love and beauty.

- Mars was named for the Roman god of war.

- Jupiter was named after the king of the Roman gods.

- Saturn was named for the Roman god of agriculture.

- Uranus was named after an ancient Greek king of the gods.

- Neptune was the Roman god of the sea.

- Pluto, which is now classified as a dwarf planet, was the Roman god of the underworld.

- The name Earth is an English/German name, which simply means *the ground*.

1. Why do you think astronomers continued to name planets after Roman gods and goddesses in more recent times?

   _____

   _____

2. From what you know about Mars, why do you think it was named for the Roman god of war?

   _____

   _____

3. Imagine you had to come up with a name for 581 c. What would you call this new planet? Explain your name choice.

   _____

   _____

A Cure for Curiosity

Maybe you aren't eager to learn how to skin a rabbit. Possibly you already know how to use Morse code. Or, perhaps you aren't a boy. Still, chances are that *The Dangerous Book for Boys* has information that will interest you—even if the title puts you off. The how-to guide has easy-to-follow instructions about more than 75 topics. They include how to build a tree fort, skip a stone, or create fireproof cloth. Already a best seller in Britain, *The Dangerous Book* recently won a top British book prize.

Brothers Conn and Hal Iggulden aimed to write the book that they wanted to read when they were boys. "We had some old books in the house with titles like *Chemical Amusements and Experiments*," says big brother Conn. "I remember endlessly looking through these [books], generally to find things that I could make explode or set on fire." Don't get the wrong idea from the title, though. As wild as it gets, *The Dangerous Book* doesn't deliver tips about how to do anything risky or unsafe.

The brothers tested all of the instructions in the book themselves. "Rule Number One was we either had to make it or do it," explains Conn. "We've both read books where the author clearly hasn't made a raft or whatever, and so the instructions don't work."

The Dangerous Book can satisfy the curiosity of any kid, so why is it written especially for boys? "It's not exactly that we are excluding girls," says Conn. "But we wanted to celebrate boys because nobody has been doing it for a long while."

A Cure for Curiosity (cont.)

Directions: Answer these questions. You may look at the article.

1. Why do you think the book is titled *The Dangerous Book for Boys* if it doesn't really have anything risky or unsafe in it?

   _____

   _____

2. Why do you think the brothers wanted to test all the instructions?

   _____

   _____

3. What do you think Conn means when he says that nobody has been "celebrating" boys lately?

   _____

   _____

4. What does it mean to skip a stone? If you don't know, take a guess.

   _____

   _____

5. Do you think it's a good idea to teach a kid how to skin a rabbit? Why or why not?

   _____

   _____

6. Imagine you are writing *The Dangerous Book for Girls*. What are three topics you think girls would be interested in?

   _____

   _____

A Cure for Curiosity (cont.)

Directions: Look at the table of contents. Answer the questions.

The Dangerous Book for Girls

Table of Contents

How to Fly a Kite..page 12

How to Bake a Cake..page 16

How to Change a Tire..page 22

How to Do a Cartwheel...page 28

How to Walk in Heels..page 33

How to Play Softball..page 37

---

1. List three things the chapter on baking a cake might include.

    _____

    _____

2. Which is the one chapter that would not make any sense to include in *The Dangerous Book for Boys*?

    _____

    _____

3. Do you think it makes sense to have separate books for boys and girls? Why or why not?

    _____

    _____

Summer Vacation Is Too Long

This summer, 50 million kids will spend their time instant messaging, watching TV, playing video games, and nagging older siblings to take them to the mall. They will also be putting their academic futures at risk.

Summer vacation once made sense—back when you didn't need an education to get a good job. Years ago, many Americans worked in manufacturing jobs that did not require a college degree but still offered a decent wage.

Things have changed. For today's students, academic skills are critical to future success. Many nations don't give kids an American-style summer vacation. They offer no more than seven consecutive weeks of vacation. Most American school districts give up to 13 weeks off. To compete in the global marketplace, Americans must be prepared to go up against international competitors.

Summer vacation also poses challenges for today's families. In the 1960s, more than 60 percent of families had a stay-at-home mom. Now, two-thirds of American children live in households where every adult works. For these families, summer vacation can be more burden than break. Someone must watch the kids.

Experts have found that during the summer, some students forget what they have learned. And though there are schools in the United States with year-round calendars, only five percent of kids go to those schools.

A longer school year wouldn't necessarily be bad news for students. It would allow time-pressed teachers to conduct richer and more imaginative lessons. Schools would have more time to devote to sports, languages, music, and the arts.

Summer vacation can be a grand thing. But in the 21st century, it may also be outdated.

Summer Vacation Is Too Long (cont.)

Directions: Answer these questions. You may look at the article.

1. What is the writer's opinion about summer vacations?

   _____

   _____

2. What do you think is the writer's strongest argument against summer breaks? Explain your answer.

   _____

   _____

3. What is the writer's weakest argument? Why do you think that?

   _____

   _____

4. Why do so many more United States households need to have babysitters during the summer than they used to?

   _____

   _____

5. According to the writer, why might some kids wind up enjoying being in school during the summer months?

   _____

   _____

6. Do you think seven weeks off during the summer would be enough for you? Why or why not?

   _____

   _____

Summer Vacation Is Too Long (cont.)

Directions: Look at the calendar below. Answer the questions.

Hawaii's New School Calendar

The state of Hawaii has created a public school calendar that shortens the summer break to seven weeks. However, it features other breaks throughout the year:

July 25	Teachers return for work
July 27	First day for students
Oct. 2–6	Fall recess
Dec. 21–Jan. 10	Winter recess
March 19–30	Spring recess
June 8	Last day of school

1. Besides the summer break, what is students' longest break during the year?

   _____

   _____

2. What do you think of this calendar? Do you think it's a better schedule than your school district has now? Why or why not?

   _____

   _____

3. If you could design a school calendar with 13 weeks off during the year, how would you plan it?

   _____

   _____

An Underwater Treasure Trove

Deep in the Atlantic Ocean, explorers have found what may be the most valuable sunken treasure in history. A company called Odyssey Marine Exploration announced that its deep-sea divers had raised 17 tons of colonial-era coins from a shipwreck in the sea. The more than 500,000 silver and gold pieces were flown by cargo jet to a secret location in the United States, where they are being examined by experts.

The coins have an estimated value of $500 million. According to rare coin expert Nick Bruyer, some coins may earn the treasure hunters several hundred dollars. But others will bring in many thousands of dollars. A coin's value is based on its condition and rarity, as well as the story behind it.

Until now, the most valuable shipwreck discovery was made in 1985 in the waters near the Florida Keys by treasure-hunter Mel Fisher. The coins and loot he found in a sunken 17th-century Spanish galleon were worth a reported $400 million.

Odyssey has not released many details about the sunken treasure. The project has been given the name Black Swan. The location of the ship and its country of origin remain unknown to the public. According to the company's co-chairman Greg Stemm, there is still uncertainty about the ship's nationality, size, and age. Court records show that the treasure might have come from a 17th-century merchant ship that sank off the coast of England. Bruyer believes the discovery is the largest of its kind. "I don't know of anything equal or comparable to it," he said.

An Underwater Treasure Trove (cont.)

Directions: Answer these questions. You may look at the article.

1. What did Odyssey Marine Exploration divers discover?

   _____

   _____

2. Why do you think details of the discovery were kept secret at first?

   _____

   _____

3. What name has the project been given?

   _____

   _____

4. How do experts estimate how much a coin is worth?

   _____

   _____

5. How much do experts think the coins found in this treasure are worth?

   _____

   _____

6. Where and when was the last most valuable shipwreck discovery made?

   _____

   _____

7. What kind of ship do researchers think the new treasure may have come from? How did they determine that?

   _____

   _____

An Underwater Treasure Trove (cont.)

Directions: Look at the map and read the caption. Answer the questions.

The Shipwreck of the *S.S. Republic*

In 2003, Odyssey Marine Exploration discovered the shipwreck of the *S.S. Republic*. It was a side-wheel steamer lost in deep water in 1865 after battling a hurricane for two days. The ship, en route from New York to New Orleans, was reportedly carrying $400,000 in gold when it sank. The ship's fascinating history includes service in both the Confederate and Union navies during the Civil War.

The shipwreck was found nearly 1,700 feet below the surface of the Atlantic Ocean about 100 miles off the Georgia coast. A team of divers recovered about 14,000 artifacts and 51,000 coins.

1. What three states are illustrated on the map?

   _____

   _____

2. What does the X in the sea indicate?

   _____

   _____

3. How did the *S.S. Republic* sink?

   _____

   _____

4. What do the *S.S. Republic* and the shipwreck in the first article have in common?

   _____

   _____

Power Baker

Blowtorches, power saws, and explosives aren't typical tools of the trade for a pastry chef. But then, Duff Goldman is not your typical baker.

Goldman, 31, is the owner of Charm City Cakes in Baltimore, Maryland. He is also the extreme-cake chef on the Food Network's series Ace of Cakes. Goldman has baked a replica of Wrigley Field baseball stadium, a seven-tiered Cat in the Hat wedding cake, a three-foot-tall sea horse, and a car engine with exploding fireworks. His edible creations take between 10 and 200 hours to assemble. They range in price from $175 to $20,000.

"There's a lot of construction involved," Goldman says. "We have every tool you can possibly imagine." For the car engine, he and his staff packed firework explosives into plastic piping and wood. Then they assembled the cake around the pipe. "We shot it off and ate it," he says.

At age 14, Goldman took his first food-industry job at a local McDonald's. "They will teach you all the skills you need to know," he says. "It's a really good first job. I would recommend it to any aspiring chef." Goldman studied history and philosophy in college. After attending cooking school in northern California, he took several pastry positions at restaurants. In 2000, he started his own business.

Goldman credits both work experience and education as key ingredients of his success. Knowledge of art, history, and even geometry are part of the mix. "People will ask for weird shapes like a hexagon," he says. Goldman draws the design or shape and uses a template to cut the cake. For this baker, cooking up a crazy cake is about much more than just flour, sugar, and power tools. "We make joy, and that makes me really happy," Goldman says. "Everything we create will make someone smile."

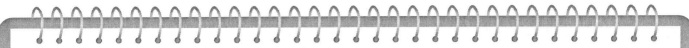

Power Baker (cont.)

Directions: Answer these questions. You may look at the article.

1. Why do you think customers might request an unusual cake?

   _____

   _____

2. Why does Goldman recommend a fast-food job for an aspiring chef?

   _____

   _____

3. Does Goldman think his college education makes him a better chef? Why or why not?

   _____

   _____

4. What did he do after attending cooking school?

   _____

   _____

5. Why do you think someone would order a cake in the shape of Wrigley Field?

   _____

   _____

6. Think of a special occasion and describe a cake creation that would be appropriate. Use lots of details.

   _____

   _____

Power Baker *(cont.)*

Directions: Look at the recipe and picture. Answer the questions.

Ladybug Cupcakes

Ingredients

- 1 cupcake
- red frosting
- 1 chocolate wafer
- black whip licorice
- 1 black gumdrop

Directions

1. Ice the cupcake with the red frosting.
2. Carefully cut the chocolate wafer into two pieces. Then cover them with dots of frosting. Support the wings with frosting on the edges of the cupcake.
3. Insert the licorice into the gumdrop head to form antennae.
4. Put the gumdrop on the cupcake.

1. How would the picture of the cupcake help you if you were making this dessert?

   _____

   _____

2. How many cupcakes does this recipe make?

   _____

   _____

3. If you were creating a cake for a beach party, what are some unusual shapes or decorations you might try?

   _____

   _____

Pals for Life

In 1999, Ryan Hreljac and Jimmy Akana became pen pals. They lived on two continents, thousands of miles apart. Their lives could not have been more different. Ryan lived with his family in Kemptville, Canada. Jimmy, an orphan, lived in Agweo, Uganda. Jimmy's life was in constant danger because rebel troops would raid his village. Fate, and Ryan's determination to help others, brought the pals together.

When Ryan was 6, he learned that millions of people in Africa did not have access to clean water. He decided to change that. To raise money, Ryan did chores for four months. He earned $70, but that was not enough to build even one well. "I realized that I couldn't raise $2,000 by doing chores," he said. "So I started doing public speaking." So far, the Ryan's Well Foundation has built 238 wells in 11 countries. "We've helped almost 400,000 people and raised $1.5 million," Ryan says.

The foundation's first well was built in Agweo, where Jimmy lived. For the first time in his life, Jimmy was able to get clean drinking water without having to walk for miles. The boys met in 2000, when Ryan traveled to Uganda. "We had a connection from the beginning," says Jimmy of that meeting.

Four years ago, the Hreljac family adopted Jimmy and brought him to live in their home. Ryan, 15, and Jimmy, 17, speak to communities and schools all over the world about the importance of having clean drinking water. They tell the story of the well that brought them together in *Ryan and Jimmy*, a new book written by Herb Shoveller.

To find out how you can help Ryan and Jimmy bring safe water to more people, go to **ryanswell.ca**.

Pals for Life (cont.)

Directions: Answer these questions. You may look at the article.

1. How did Ryan and Jimmy meet?

   _____

   _____

2. Why did Ryan want to raise money?

   _____

   _____

3. How has the money been used?

   _____

   _____

4. Why do you think Ryan traveled to Uganda?

   _____

   _____

5. How did Ryan and Jimmy's relationship change from four years ago?

   _____

   _____

6. What are Ryan and Jimmy doing now to improve conditions in Africa?

   _____

   _____

7. How could you learn more about their story?

   _____

   _____

Pals for Life (cont.)

Directions: Look at the chart. Answer the questions.

How Much Water Do We Use?

Americans use more water per person than many other countries.
Here's how some countries compare.

Country	Water Consumption, per capita	Country	Water Consumption, per capita
New Zealand	177 gallons	Egypt	35 gallons
Armenia	174 gallons	Mexico	34 gallons
United Arab Emirates	150 gallons	Israel	32.5 gallons
United States	147 gallons	Greece	32.5 gallons
Canada	114 gallons	Netherlands	18 gallons
Italy	100 gallons	India	18 gallons
Japan	99 gallons	China	15 gallons
Germany	72 gallons	Morocco	14 gallons
France	68 gallons	Afghanistan	7 gallons
Brazil	67 gallons	Honduras	6.5 gallons
Libya	56 gallons	Rwanda	3.6 gallons
Finland	40.5 gallons	Mozambique	2 gallons
Tajikistan	40.5 gallons		

1. What does the phrase *per capita* mean?

_____

_____

2. Which countries use more water per capita than the United States?

_____

_____

3. What are three things your family can do at home to cut down on water usage?

_____

_____

A Writer's Journey

What do a large-eared mouse, a goofy dog, and a caged tiger have in common? All three are unlikely heroes in books by Kate DiCamillo. Another animal character takes center stage in the author's newest novel, *The Miraculous Journey of Edward Tulane*. Edward Tulane is an almost-three-foot-tall rabbit made of china. His owner, 10-year-old Abilene, loves him. She talks to him and dresses him in fine suits each day. After Abilene's family takes an ocean voyage, Edward is lost at sea. On his journey to find a home, he learns important lessons about love.

DiCamillo, 41, admits that as a child growing up in Clermont, Florida, she read everything except animal stories. "The irony is that as a kid, I wouldn't have read any of the books that I've written, because every one of them has an animal on the cover," she says. "I try to make it not happen and [the animals] show up anyway."

Readers don't mind a bit. In 2004, DiCamillo won the Newbery Medal. That's the top prize for children's writing from the American Library Association. She won it for *The Tale of Despereaux*, a story about an unusual mouse. A film based on the story is now in the works. The author's first book, *Because of Winn-Dixie*, is about a 10-year-old girl and a dog named Winn-Dixie. The award-winning book was also made into a movie.

DiCamillo says she writes two pages a day, five days a week. As she writes, she doesn't even think about the age of her readers. Her books are for everyone. Says DiCamillo: "I think of myself as a storyteller, and stories don't know any age."

A Writer's Journey (cont.)

Directions: Answer these questions. You may look at the article.

1. Why does DiCamillo say that it's *ironic* that animals are the main characters in her books?

   _____

   _____

2. What makes Edward Tulane unusual?

   _____

   _____

3. What honor did DiCamillo win for her writing? Which book did she win it for?

   _____

   _____

4. Which of her books is already a movie, and which one is being made into a movie?

   _____

   _____

5. Which do you think is better: reading a book and then watching the movie based on it, or watching the movie first, and then reading the book? Explain your answer.

   _____

   _____

6. Why do you think people of all ages like DiCamillo's books?

   _____

   _____

7. How many pages does DiCamillo write most weeks?

   _____

   _____

A Writer's Journey (cont.)

Directions: Read the list below. Answer the questions.

Tips for Writing

Kate DiCamillo offers these tips for those who are interested in becoming writers:

1. **Write**—This may seem like an obvious piece of advice, but there are a lot of people who think that somehow they can become a writer without doing the work of writing. Make a commitment to write a little bit (a paragraph, a page, two pages) every day.

2. **Rewrite**—You can't sit down and expect something beautiful and wise to spring forth from your fingers the first time you write. You can, however, reasonably expect a piece of writing to get better each time you rewrite it. Writing means rewriting.

3. **Read**—You have no business wanting to be a writer unless you are a reader. Read fantasies and essays, biographies and poetry, fables and fairy tales. Read, read, read, read, read.

4. **Look**—Pay attention to the details in the world around you.

5. **Listen**—Everyone has a story. Listen to people when they talk. Eavesdrop. Join in conversations. Ask questions.

6. **Believe in Yourself**—There is no right or wrong way to tell a story. This is one reason that writing is so wonderful and terrifying: you have to find your own way.

---

1. What do you think are the three most valuable tips that DiCamillo offers to beginning writers? Explain your answer.

   _____

   _____

2. Why do you think it's so important for good writers to be readers?

   _____

   _____

3. Which of these tips do you think you might be able to use to become a better writer? How would you do it?

   _____

   _____

Bad News for Bees

Beekeepers, researchers, and farmers are all abuzz about a mysterious wave of disappearances. Millions of honeybees are vanishing, leaving no clues, and no dead bodies behind.

Experts have a name for the honeybees' disappearing act: Colony Collapse Disorder (CCD). Two dozen states have reported CCD. In North Dakota and California, the nation's top honey-producing states, honey production is way down. North Dakota's output dropped 23 percent from last year and California's plummeted by 34 percent.

Honeybees are hardworking insects. Of course, they produce honey. Along with birds, bats, and other insects, honeybees are also among nature's most important pollinators. Bees pollinate flowering plants by moving tiny grains of pollen from one part of a flower to another so that a plant can grow seeds and fruit. Bee pollination is crucial for crops like apples, almonds, cucumbers, and cranberries. "At least a third of what we eat is pollinated by insects, primarily honeybees," says Bromenshenk. Technology cannot duplicate this delicate work. It must be done by bees. "There are fewer bees to pollinate the crops that you eat every day," says Bromenshenk. "People are worried."

Experts say the disappearance could be a result of a disease similar to one that devastated the country's bee population several years ago. Another possibility is that honeybees are reacting to a harmful pesticide. The National Honey Board and other groups connected to the bee biz are giving emergency funds to support the research and try to stop the crisis. If the cause of CCD is identified soon, beekeepers may be able to protect their hives. Then everyone will see if the bees can bounce back.

Bad News for Bees (cont.)

Directions: Answer these questions. You may look at the article.

1. What is the name of the disorder that researchers have given the bees' disappearance?

   _____

   _____

2. How many states have reported the problem?

   _____

   _____

3. Why are researchers so worried?

   _____

   _____

4. How has the problem affected their honey production?

   _____

   _____

5. What other animals pollinate plants?

   _____

   _____

6. What are two theories for the bees' disappearance?

   _____

   _____

7. What is being done to find a solution?

   _____

   _____

Bad News for Bees (cont.)

Directions: Many fruit and vegetable plants are pollinated by honeybees. Look at the diagram to learn how this process works. Then answer the questions below.

STIGMA   ANTHER

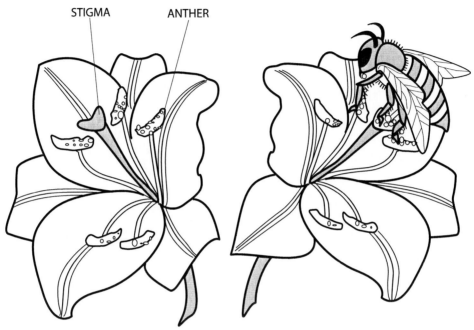

The honeybee visits the flower to get pollen and nectar for food. Some pollen sticks to the hair on the honeybee's legs. The honeybee visits another flower. Some pollen falls off its legs onto the flower's stigma. Now the flower can make seeds.

Pollen from the anther of one flower is moved to the stigma of another flower.

1. How does the honeybee get pollen from one flower to another?

   _____

   _____

2. The hair on a honeybee's hind legs is sometimes called a pollen basket. Why do you think this is?

   _____

   _____

3. Wind can also move pollen from one flower to another. Which do you think is more efficient at pollinating plants, the wind or the honeybee? Explain your answer.

   _____

   _____

She's Serious About Comics

Drawing is Alexa Kitchen's favorite hobby. She spends at least three hours a day sketching characters and creating comics. There are piles of paper all around her family's Massachusetts home. "If I draw myself into a corner and can't think of anything else, it's a reject," she says. "I keep drawing until I find something I'm happy with."

Her work has paid off. Last summer, her parents published a book of her "keepers," *Drawing Comics Is Easy! (Except When It's Hard)*. Alexa, 9, is critical of it. The comics are from when she was 7, and aren't as detailed as her recent drawings. Still, her work has drawn praise from professional cartoonists, including Patrick McDonnell, creator of the comic strip *Mutts*.

Before becoming a publisher, Alexa's father, Denis, was a cartoonist. His company released Alexa's book. Alexa shares some of her practiced pencil-to-paper tips in her book. She hopes it will help other young artists to "find their own styles."

Alexa uses her interests and activities as material for comics. One in particular, "annoying my parents," will soon get top billing. She says her father is gathering some of her work for a second book, *Grown-Ups Are Dumb*. It's about "how kids see their parents, no offense." None taken—not by Alexa's mom, Stacey, anyway: "We're just as pleased as punch she has found something she loves!" she says.

She's Serious About Comics *(cont.)*

Directions: Answer these questions. You may look at the article.

1. Why is Alexa critical of the drawings in her book?

   _____

   _____

2. Why do you think Alexa might have become interested in drawing?

   _____

   _____

3. If Alexa draws seven days a week, about how many hours per week does she draw?

   _____

   _____

4. What do you think the title of Alexa's book means?

   _____

   _____

5. How does Alexa get ideas for her comics?

   _____

   _____

6. What is the idea behind her second book?

   _____

   _____

7. What is your favorite cartoon character? What is it about that character that you like?

   _____

   _____

She's Serious About Comics (cont.)

Directions: Look at the drawings below. Answer the questions.

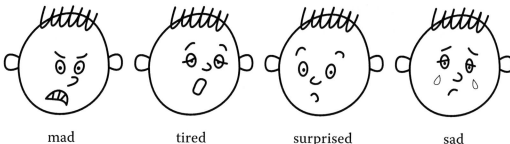

| mad | tired | surprised | sad |

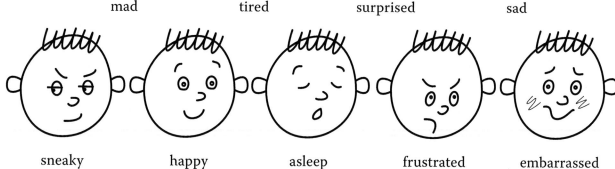

| sneaky | happy | asleep | frustrated | embarrassed |

1. What parts of the character's face change as her mood changes?

   _____

   _____

2. How do you think the artist figured out how each expression should be drawn?

   _____

   _____

3. Pretend you are a cartoonist. Describe a story you could draw in a cartoon strip that you think readers would find entertaining.

   _____

   _____

A Whole New World

Fish that change color, shrimp that look like praying mantises, and sharks that walk. No, these aren't mythical characters in an upcoming animated film. They are just a few of the new species of undersea life found off the coast of Indonesia's Papua Province.

Conservation International announced that a 12-member team of scientists has discovered 24 new species of fish, 20 species of coral, and eight species of shrimp. That makes 52 new kinds of neighbors here on Earth. The scientists were exploring a remote location known as Bird's Head Seascape. "Each site was about the size of two football fields," says Mark Erdmann, the senior adviser of Conservation International. "It was the best six weeks. Everyone on board was giddy like schoolchildren!" Among the scientists' discoveries were two types of epaulette sharks. The 3-foot-long spotted fish live in shallow water. They walk on the sea bottom, using their lower fins.

The Seascape is a remote, almost 71,000-square-mile area. It is home to 75 percent of all known coral species in the world. "It's one of the most stunningly beautiful landscapes and seascapes on the planet," says Erdmann.

Although the underwater research trips started in 2001, the scientists had to make sure that all the never-before-seen species were, in fact, new. "After you discover a new species, you must describe it in detail and have those results published in a scientific journal," says scientist Sebastian Troeng. "The species is not recognized until it passes through those steps."

The team is hoping that these discoveries will shine new light on underwater expeditions. "There is still a lot to be discovered underwater," says Erdmann. "We know more about the moon than we do about our own planet. We need to do more under water."

A Whole New World *(cont.)*

Directions: Answer these questions. You may look at the article.

1. What kinds of new species were found?

   _____

   _____

2. The size of the Seascape was described two ways. How was it described, and which way better helped you to visualize the size of the area?

   _____

   _____

3. What are two other things you learned about the Seascape?

   _____

   _____

4. What makes the shark that was found so unusual?

   _____

   _____

5. How long were scientists exploring the Seascape?

   _____

   _____

6. Why did it take so long for scientists to announce their discovery?

   _____

   _____

7. What does Erdmann compare underwater exploration to?

   _____

   _____

A Whole New World (cont.)

Directions: Look at the map. Answer the questions.

Bird's Head Seascape

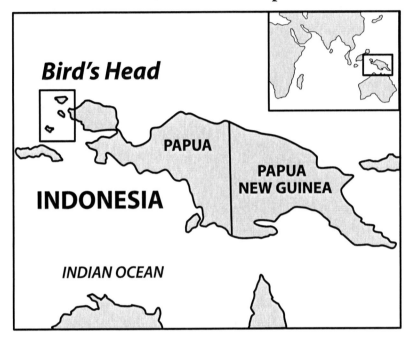

1. Why does this illustration show both the wider world map and a map of Indonesia?

   _____

   _____

2. Why do you think the area might have been named Bird's Head?

   _____

   _____

3. There are plans to protect Bird's Head from overfishing. Why do you think the group's expedition helped increase efforts to protect the region?

   _____

   _____

Mr. Mix-It

Maelo Cordova spends his day shaping Play-Doh, trying out Barbie makeup, and racing Hot Wheels cars. Surprisingly, Cordova is not a kid. He's a chemist. At his job, he uses his knowledge of chemistry to make toys.

Cordova is one of thousands of chemists around the country who hopes to get kids interested in science. National Chemistry Week is October 16 through 22. All week, these scientists will talk about how chemistry is used in toy making.

As a kid in Puerto Rico, Cordova wondered what exactly is in shampoo that helps it clean hair. He also experimented—mixing cleaning products, for example, to get out spots. In high school, Cordova discovered the name of his hobby: chemistry. He loved learning how substances combine to make new stuff. After winning a top science award, he studied chemistry in college. He now works at the Mattel toy company.

At work, Cordova mixes chemicals and performs experiments. But he does his homework first. "I like to spend time investigating what I'm looking for before I get in the lab," Cordova explains. For one project, he was asked to make icky, sticky play slime. His recipe was a little off. The goo came out harder than he wanted, and he almost tossed it into the trash. Instead, he saved the substance and went on to earn a patent for Flubber, his new invention. Says Cordova: "In science, you never throw anything away." His next mistake may turn out to be even more fun.

Mr. Mix-It (cont.)

Directions: Answer these questions. You may look at the article.

1. How did Cordova become interested in chemistry?

   _____

   _____

2. Why do toy companies need chemists on their staff?

   _____

   _____

3. What company does Cordova work for?

   _____

   _____

4. Why do you think it helps for him to investigate his experiments before he gets into the lab?

   _____

   _____

5. What toy did his mistake become?

   _____

   _____

6. What is the goal of National Chemistry Week?

   _____

   _____

7. What other kinds of things do you use every day that are made by chemists?

   _____

   _____

Mr. Mix-It *(cont.)*

Directions: Look at the recipe. Answer the questions.

Make Your Own Flubber!

Materials

Container 1

$\frac{3}{4}$ cup warm water

1 cup white glue

food coloring (a few drops)

Container 2

$\frac{1}{2}$ cup warm water

2 teaspoons Borax

Directions

1. Thoroughly mix ingredients in each container.

2. Pour container 2 into container 1. No need to stir, just reach in and pull out a glob of Flubber!

---

1. How many ingredients do you need for Flubber?

   _____

   _____

2. Are there any ingredients that you think you would not have at home? Which ones? Where do you think you would be able to get them?

   _____

   _____

3. Think of something you have enjoyed playing with that was the result of a chemist working at a toy company. Describe the toy and explain how you think it might have been made.

   _____

   _____

References Cited

Grigg, W. S., M. C. Daane, Y. Jin, and J. R. Campbell. 2003. National assessment of educational progress. The nation's report card: Reading 2002. Washington, DC: U.S. Department of Education.

Gulek, C. 2003. Preparing for high-stakes testing. *Theory into Practice* 42 (1): 42–50.

Ivey, G., and K. Broaddus. 2000. Tailoring the fit: Reading instruction and middle school readers. *The Reading Teacher* 54 (1): 68–78.

Kletzien, S. B. 1998. Information text or narrative text? Children's preferences revisited. Paper presented at the National Reading Conference, Austin, TX.

Miller, D. 2002. *Reading with meaning: Teaching comprehension in the primary grades.* Portland, ME: Stenhouse.

Moss, B. and J. Hendershot. 2002. Exploring sixth graders' selection of nonfiction trade books. *The Reading Teacher* 56 (1): 6–18.

Pardo, L. S. 2002. Book club for the twenty-first century. *Illinois Reading Council Journal* 30 (4): 14–23.

RAND Reading Study Group. 2002. Reading for understanding: Toward a research and development program in reading comprehension. Santa Monica, CA: Office of Education Research and Improvement.

U.S. Congress. House. *No Child Left Behind Act of 2001.* Pub. L. No. 107–110, 115 Stat. 1425 (2002).

Student Achievement Graph

Passage Title	# of Questions	Number of Questions Correctly Answered						
		1	2	3	4	5	6	7

Answer Key

Many of the answers will show an example of how the students might respond. For many of the questions there may be more than one correct answer.

Page 19

1. The Bronx Zoo is the largest city zoo in the United States.
2. Zookeepers, veterinarians, a nutritionist, and many others work to keep the animals healthy and happy.
3. Responses will vary, but may include treating animals.
4. Answers may vary.
5. Answers may vary.
6. Answers may vary.
7. Answers may vary.

Page 20

1. any three of the following recipe ingredients: carrots, beans, pears, apples, blueberries, grapes, beans, corn
2. Responses may vary, but may include that the ingredients are mostly vegetables and fruits.
3. Responses will vary; recipes may include bananas.

Page 22

1. Edmund Hillary and Tenzing Norgay
2. At least 175 men and women have died.
3. Nearly 1,200 climbers have reached the top.
4. Responses will vary, but may include warm clothing, climbing gear, and food.
5. Answers may vary.
6. Answers may vary.
7. Answers may vary.

Page 23

1. Mt. Everest is the tallest at 29,035 feet. Mt. Cook is the shortest at 12,254 feet.

Page 23 *(cont.)*

2. Responses will vary, but may include that climbers can use the chart to predict the level of climbing difficulty based on the mountain's height and location. The locations and names of the mountains could also be useful.
3. Answers may vary.

Page 25

1. The characters are in books and movies.
2. No, it's not easy.
3. Filmmakers have to fit long books into two-hour movies or short books need to be expanded.
4. Answers may vary.
5. Answers may vary.
6. Answers may vary.
7. Answers may vary.

Page 26

1. Answers may vary.
2. Answers may vary.
3. Answers may vary.

Page 28

1. Christine King Farris wrote about growing up with Martin.
2. They made the neighbors think their grandmother's fur piece was a wild animal.
3. Answers may vary.
4. Answers may vary.
5. Answers may vary.
6. Answers may vary.

Page 29

Students will write a letter. Answers may vary.

Page 31

1. They are elephants that create works of art.
2. The money is used to support an elephant conservation center.
3. In 1989 when logging stopped, the elephants lost their jobs carrying logs.
4. Vitaly Komar and Alex Melamid set up elephant art schools and brought attention to Thai elephants.
5. Responses will vary, but may include that they are both elephant artists. They are different because they paint in different styles and colors.
6. Answers may vary.
7. Answers may vary.

Page 32

1. It shows how few elephants are left in Asia.
2. India
3. These animals face threats from hunting, habitat loss, and human populations moving into wildlife areas.

Page 34

1. the fossil of a 40-foot-long crocodile
2. It was as long as a school bus and weighed as much as a small whale.
3. emperor
4. It had a five-foot-long jaw and more than 100 teeth, making it big enough to eat a dinosaur.
5. Its eye sockets were angled so that it could look for prey from underwater.
6. Armorlike bony plates covered its body and protected it from attacks.

Answer Key (cont.)

Page 34 (cont.)

7. Responses will vary, but may include that the crocodile was able to adapt to its changing surroundings better than dinosaurs could.

Page 35

1. Responses will vary, but may include that the illustrations helped the student visualize the size of the croc.

2. It helps us visualize something if it is compared to something else that we all understand.

3. Responses will vary, but may include a school bus because that was used in the article as a comparison.

Page 37

1. She had to drop out of school in first grade, so she has to make up for lost time.

2. Her family was poor and she had to work.

3. Boys are more likely to get paying jobs when they get older, so parents send them to school.

4. Campaign for Female Education; It pays for girls to go to school.

5. Public school is free for families in the United States because it is supported by the taxes we pay the government.

6. A better-educated society is able to solve their own communities' problems, start businesses, and help to end poverty.

Page 38

1. It shows how an early education helps throughout a woman's life and strengthens her community.

2. A girl completes primary education.

Page 38 (cont.)

3. Responses will vary, but may include that a girl who starts school is more likely to continue because she enjoys learning and sees it as leading to a brighter future.

4. Responses will vary, but may include that a woman with a good education is more likely to have daughters who continue the cycle of education and achievement.

Page 40

1. A telescope's power depends largely on the size of the mirror inside it.

2. Older telescopes had thick, heavy mirrors, but there were limits to how big they could be. Some new scopes have thin, flexible mirrors controlled by computers.

3. Answers will vary, but may include that they have views of the night sky that are unobstructed by buildings or city lights.

4. The Keck telescope has a jumbo mirror (33 feet across) made up of many small ones. It is located in Hawaii.

5. A new telescope in Chile helped scientists estimate that the age of the universe is 14 billion years.

6. He discovered 35 planets circling sunlike stars.

7. Answers may vary.

Page 41

1. two

2. reflecting telescope, because it includes mirrors

3. Answers may vary.

Page 41 (cont.)

4. Responses will vary, but may include that the diagram shows how light is reflected off the mirror on the reflecting telescope and how refracting telescopes use lenses to enlarge images for the viewer.

Page 43

1. Each year, 5 million kids are bullied.

2. Responses will vary, but may include that some kids may be bullied at home, so they bully other kids when they get to school.

3. At first he ignores the bully, and then he tells a teacher.

4. She got bullied for getting good grades.

5. Answers may vary.

6. Answers may vary.

7. Answers may vary.

Page 44

1. Answers may vary.

2. Answers may vary.

3. Answers may vary.

4. Answers may vary.

Page 46

1. The city was built on marshy land in a lagoon, and climate changes have caused seawaters to rise.

2. It is a beautiful city built on 118 islands, where canals serve as streets and boats serve as taxis. It is also the home of beautiful buildings and artwork.

3. The seawater has damaged art treasures and historic sites.

4. Some experts say Venice will sink 8 inches in the next 50 years.

5. a $2 billion plan to stop the flooding

Answer Key *(cont.)*

Page 46 *(cont.)*

6. The group wants to place huge underwater gates at the three entrances to the Venice lagoon. The gates would act as dams and hold back the seawater.

7. Critics argue that by shutting out seawater, the gates would harm the lagoon's fish and plant life.

Page 47

1. two

2. back to the sea

3. Answers may vary.

Page 49

1. Rooseveltown, New York; it was started by parents of students.

2. the language of Mohawk Indians

3. They are happy they are learning it.

4. It is an area that the government has set aside for Native Americans.

5. The Mohawk language was disappearing and parents wanted their children to learn it.

6. They learn old Mohawk songs and dances.

7. Answers may vary.

Page 50

1. Answers may vary.

2. Answers may vary.

3. Responses will vary, but may include that the list of common words would allow someone to communicate in a limited way fairly quickly, while the alphabet shows the reader the foundation of the language.

Page 52

1. Do you search the Internet in the snow and rain?

2. a living, growing thing

3. As the world changes, we need new words to describe it.

Page 52 *(cont.)*

4. every year

5. every 10 years; 10,000 words

6. catalogs and comic books

7. a type of e-mail and meat

Page 53

1. Answers may vary.

2. Answers may vary.

Page 55

1. It means that because of rising tooth decay rates, more young children will be losing their teeth earlier than usual.

2. Tooth decay in baby teeth rose from 24 percent to 28 percent in children ages 2 to 5. It surprised researchers because before that, tooth decay had been on the decline for 40 years.

3. Experts blame it on children eating more processed snack foods and drinking bottled water.

4. Bottled water does not contain fluoride.

5. A serious form of gum disease called periodontitis has decreased by 50 percent in adults 20 to 64 years old.

6. Answers may vary.

Page 56

1. enamel

2. The visible part of the tooth is called the crown.

3. The cementum, nerves, and blood vessels and root end opening are below the gum line. When you have a toothache, the nerves transmit pain to the brain.

Page 58

1. The African city of Mwinda has floating farms, hydrogen-powered hover vehicles, and renewable energy resources for the city's power.

Page 58 *(cont.)*

2. All the cities were powered by fuel-cell technology.

3. Many national contests are held in Washington, D.C. because it is our nation's capital.

4. Responses will vary, but may include meeting with teachers and volunteer engineer mentors, or creating a fictional city on *SimCity 3000*.

5. They presented their creation to a panel of judges.

6. Answers may vary.

Page 59

1. Answers may vary.

2. Answers may vary.

3. Answers may vary.

Page 61

1. Organizers hoped the academy would be a positive force in the community and get kids excited about baseball.

2. Former major leaguers teach baseball to the kids. They probably volunteer to give back to the community.

3. No, because many of them may not have been able to afford to go to a major league baseball game.

4. Organizers want kids to know how important school is to their success.

5. Answers may vary.

6. Responses will vary, but may include that it is fair because these kids may not have had the same opportunities as kids growing up in better neighborhoods.

Page 62

1. The story is about a baseball academy, and the illustration shows a baseball field.

Answer Key (cont.)

Page 62 *(cont.)*

2. nine

3. Answers may vary.

Page 64

1. the 50 State Quarters program

2. They will come out in the order in which each president served.

3. He probably wanted to show that the coins have a practical use and can fit in parking meters.

4. Responses will vary, but may include that the United States Mint usually issues special series of coins over time so that collectors can build their collections gradually.

5. Responses will vary, but may include that coins are heavier to carry than bills.

6. Answers may vary.

Page 65

1. Responses will vary, but may include that all are round, are worth $1, and have *United States of America* on the back.

2. Responses will vary, but may include that the Susan B. Anthony coin does not have a smooth edge; there is the Statue of Liberty instead of a bald eagle on the back of the presidential coin; and that the presidential coin is part of a collection.

3. Answers may vary.

Page 67

1. Autrey is compared to Superman because both are considered heroes.

2. Hollopeter probably would have been killed by an oncoming train.

3. They were probably very scared of what might happen to their father.

Page 67 *(cont.)*

4. He received the Bronze Medallion from Mayor Bloomberg, $10,000 from Donald Trump, a trip to Disney World, and one year of free subway rides.

5. Answers may vary.

6. Answers may vary.

Page 68

1. Responses will vary, but should include 1, 4, 7, 10.

2. Responses will vary, but should include 2, 3, 5, 6, 8, 9.

3. Answers may vary.

4. Answers may vary.

Page 70

1. It is so rare; there were only five giant pandas born at United States zoos in the last six years.

2. The Atlanta Zoo held an online poll to name the panda.

3. Mei Lan, translated to Atlanta Beauty, probably appealed to a lot of people who go to the Atlanta Zoo.

4. The father might present a danger to the baby panda.

5. They live in the mountains to escape the development that threatens their habitat.

6. Most pandas in captivity live in China; this is because pandas are native to China.

7. Americans don't get many opportunities to see pandas because there are so few at zoos in the United States.

Page 71

1. An omnivore is an animal that eats both meat and vegetables.

2. American black bear, because it is listed as "common" on the chart.

Page 71 *(cont.)*

3. The bear population is likely to shrink because the habitats of the sun bear, sloth bear, and polar bear are all threatened.

Page 73

1. This is the first time scientists have discovered a planet outside our solar system that could sustain life. That means there could be extraterrestrial life.

2. gravity

3. Water is the basis of all life. No plant or animal can survive without it.

4. This refers to the fairy tale *Goldilocks and the Three Bears*. In the story, Goldilocks preferred the smallest bear's bowl, chair, and bed, which were "just right."

5. It is too far away; you wouldn't be able to get there in a human lifetime. No humans have been able to travel outside of our solar system.

6. On a treasure map, the X usually represents where the treasure is buried.

7. Answers may vary.

Page 74

1. Responses will vary, but may include that they probably wanted the planets' names to be consistent.

2. It was probably named for the god of war because of its fiery red color.

3. Answers may vary.

Page 76

1. Responses will vary, but may include that the authors probably thought the name would appeal to adventurous boys.

2. They wanted to see if everything would work; answers may vary.

Answer Key (cont.)

Page 76 (cont.)

3. Responses will vary, but may include that he doesn't think that boys get as much recognition as girls do.

4. It involves throwing a stone with a flattened surface across a lake or other body of water in such a way that it bounces off the surface of the water. The object of the game is to see how many times a stone can be made to bounce before sinking.

5. Answers may vary.

6. Answers may vary.

Page 77

1. Responses will vary, but may include preheating the oven to the correct temperature, mixing the ingredients in a bowl, and pouring the batter into a pan.

2. How to Walk in Heels

3. Answers may vary.

Page 79

1. The writer believes summer vacations are outdated.

2. Answers may vary.

3. Answers may vary.

4. More households have both parents working today.

5. Teachers would have more time to devote to more imaginative lessons, as well as sports, languages, music, and the arts.

6. Answers may vary.

Page 80

1. winter recess

2. Answers may vary.

3. Answers may vary.

Page 82

1. 17 tons of colonial-era coins from a shipwreck in the Atlantic

2. The company's owners probably don't want others to know the location of the ship yet because they don't want other divers looking for it.

Page 82 (cont.)

3. Black Swan

4. A coin's value is based on its condition and rarity, as well as the story behind it.

5. $500 million

6. in the waters near the Florida Keys in 1985

7. a 17th-century merchant ship that sank off the coast of England; researchers determined this by looking at court records

Page 83

1. South Carolina, Georgia, and Florida

2. where the shipwreck was found

3. It was lost in deep water after battling a hurricane for two days.

4. Responses will vary, but may include that they were both recovered by Odyssey Marine Exploration and that they both held valuable treasures.

Page 85

1. People like to celebrate special events with unique desserts that reflect their hobbies and interests, or just make them happy.

2. He says it teaches you the basics of cooking.

3. Yes, because sometimes he uses his knowledge of different subjects to create his designs.

4. He worked as a pastry chef at several restaurants before starting his own business.

5. The person might be a big Chicago baseball fan.

6. Answers may vary.

Page 86

1. It would help you visualize what the cupcake should look like when it's done.

2. one

3. Answers may vary.

Page 88

1. They became pen pals through Ryan's efforts to bring clean water to Jimmy's village. They met after Ryan traveled to Uganda.

2. He wanted to raise money to build wells to bring clean water to the people of Africa.

3. The money is being used to build wells throughout Africa.

4. He wanted to meet his pen pal, Jimmy, and see how the wells were improving people's lives.

5. Ryan's family adopted Jimmy and he came to live with them.

6. They are speaking out in communities and schools all over the world about the importance of having clean drinking water.

7. You could read the book about them, *Ryan and Jimmy*, or visit ryanswell.ca.

Page 89

1. per person

2. New Zealand, Armenia, and United Arab Emirates

3. Answers may vary.

Page 91

1. It's ironic because she never liked animal stories growing up.

2. He is a three-foot-tall rabbit made of china, who wears suits.

3. She won the Newberry Medal for *The Tale of Despereaux.*

4. *Because of Winn-Dixie* is already a movie; *The Tale of Despereaux* is being made into a movie.

5. Answers may vary.

6. She doesn't think about the age of her readers when she is writing, so her books appeal to everyone.

7. 10

Answer Key *(cont.)*

Page 92

1. Answers may vary.
2. Responses will vary, but may include that readers develop a better vocabulary and learn storytelling techniques they can use.
3. Answers may vary.

Page 94

1. Colony Collapse Disorder
2. two dozen, or 24
3. Honeybee pollination is crucial for crops; at least a third of what we eat is pollinated by insects, primarily honeybees.
4. North Dakota's honey output dropped 23 percent from last year, and California's dropped by 34 percent.
5. birds, bats, and other insects
6. Experts say it could be a result of a disease similar to one that devastated the country's bee population several years ago. Another theory is that honeybees are reacting to a harmful pesticide.
7. The National Honey Board and other groups connected to the bee industry are giving emergency funds to support the research and try to stop the crisis.

Page 95

1. When the honeybee visits a flower to get pollen and nectar for food, pollen sticks to the hair on its legs. When the honeybee visits another flower, some of the pollen falls off its legs, and that flower is able to make seeds.
2. Because it picks up pollen in one flower and then carries it to be deposited in another flower.
3. The honeybee is more efficient, because it drops the pollen right into the flower's stigma.

Page 97

1. Because she did the drawings when she was just seven.
2. She might have become interested in drawing because her father was a cartoonist.
3. 21
4. Responses will vary, but may include that she might mean that drawing comics sometimes is easy and sometimes is hard.
5. She uses her interests and activities as ideas for her comics.
6. It is about how kids sometimes see their parents as "dumb."
7. Answers may vary.

Page 98

1. eyes, eyebrows, mouth
2. Responses will vary, but may include from observing people.
3. Answers may vary.

Page 100

1. 24 new species of fish, 20 species of coral, and eight species of shrimp.
2. the size of two football fields; a 71,000-square-mile area. It's easier to visualize the size in terms of football fields; answers may vary.
3. Responses will vary, but might include that the Seascape is home to 75 percent of all known coral species in the world, and that it is located off the coast of Indonesia's Papua Province.
4. It walks on the sea bottom, using its lower fins.
5. for six weeks
6. They had to make sure that all the species they found really were new, and they had to have their findings published in a scientific journal.
7. moon exploration

Page 101

1. Answers may vary. Answers might include that the illustration attempts to show where Indonesia is in relation to the rest of the world.
2. The peninsula is shaped like a bird's head.
3. The area warranted better protection after researchers showed how many new species were located there.

Page 103

1. He was curious to find out how substances combine to make new stuff and started experimenting on his own.
2. Many toys, such as Play-Doh and Flubber, are invented in labs.
3. Mattel
4. It probably makes his experiments in the lab more productive because he better understands the substances he's working with.
5. Flubber
6. to get kids interested in science and chemistry
7. Responses will vary, but may include shampoo, soap, and cleaning supplies.

Page 104

1. four
2. Responses will vary, but may include borax. You could get all the ingredients at a supermarket.
3. Answers may vary.